TRAVELING
the
Freedom Road

From Slavery & the Civil War Through Reconstruction

ISAAC and ROSA, Emancipated Slave Children,
From the Free Schools of Louisiana,
Photographed by KIMBALL, 477 Broadway. N.Y.
Entered according to Act of Congress, in the year 1863 by GEO. H.
HANKS. in the Clerk's Office of the U. S. for the Sou. Dist. of N.Y.

Isaac and Rosa, the children on this card, had been enslaved in Louisiana. They were freed by President Abraham Lincoln's Emancipation Proclamation, since they lived in territory controlled by the United States (Union) Army in 1863. This photograph was taken in New York City. Copies of this card were likely sold to raise money to help newly freed slaves.

TRAVELING the Freedom Road

From Slavery & the Civil War Through Reconstruction

Linda Barrett Osborne

Published in association with
THE LIBRARY OF CONGRESS

ABRAMS BOOKS FOR YOUNG READERS
New York

*To all children
who suffer from prejudice and endure war*
—L.B.O.

Library of Congress Cataloging-in-Publication Data

Osborne, Linda Barrett, 1949–
Traveling the freedom road : from slavery and the Civil War through Reconstruction /
by Linda Barrett Osborne ; in association with the Library of Congress.
p. cm.
ISBN 978-0-8109-8338-0
1. African Americans—History—To 1863. 2. African Americans—History—1863–1877.
3. Slaves—United States—History—19th century. 4. Slavery—United States—History—19th century.
5. United States—History—Civil War, 1861–1865—African Americans. 6. Reconstruction (U.S. history,
1865–1877) 7. United States—Politics and government—1783–1865. 8. United States—Politics and
government—1865–1877. 9. U.S. states—Politics and government—19th century. I. Library of Congress.
II. Title.
E185.18.O83 2009
973.7'415—dc22
2008022298

Copyright © 2009 The Library of Congress
Book design by Maria T. Middleton
For image credits, please see page 123.

Printed and bound in U.S.A.
10 9 8 7 6 5 4 3 2 1

Abrams Books for Young Readers are available at special discounts when purchased in quantity for
premiums and promotions as well as fundraising or educational use. Special editions can also be created to
specification. For details, contact specialmarkets@hnabooks.com or the address below.

HNA ■■■■■
harry n. abrams, inc.
a subsidiary of La Martinière Groupe
115 West 18th Street
New York, NY 10011
www.hnabooks.com

CONTENTS

Fannie Virginia Casseopia Lawrence was five years old when Northern abolitionists at Henry Ward Beecher's church purchased her freedom. Fannie's skin was very light, and she likely had white ancestors. A child could have very little African American ancestry (perhaps only a grandparent or great-grandparent) and still be a slave if born to a mother who was enslaved.

PREFACE

The Library of Congress is a rare and rich place to work. In its vast collections on slavery and the Civil War, I read an essay by Marietta Hill, a student at Myrtilla Miner's School for Free Colored Girls in Washington, D.C., in the 1850s. "I think there will be blood shed before all can be free," Hill wrote, "and the question is, are we willing to give up our lives for it?" This seemed both poignant and unhappily accurate in its predictions for the future, yet it was written not by a teacher, but by a girl. I began to explore other sources at the Library to look for texts and photographs that described a young person's thoughts and experiences during the years from about 1800 to 1877, the end of Reconstruction.

Traveling the Freedom Road is a result of this research. It draws on diaries, narratives by runaway slaves, schoolwork, anti-slavery publications, and other material written by, for, and about young people during the nineteenth century. It also uses interviews conducted with former slaves in the 1930s as part of the Federal Writers' Project. Those interviewed—children and teenagers during the time of slavery, the Civil War, and Reconstruction—recounted their memories of what it felt like to be a young person toiling as a slave, surviving wartime, or gaining rights and going to school for the first time after 1865. In addition, there are quotes and stories from adults, many of them abolitionists, which convey information and observations that complement the youthful perspective.

The history of the first eight decades of the nineteenth century is extraordinarily complex and varied. *Traveling the Freedom Road* is too small in scope to convey this complexity or to comprehensively cover every aspect of these years, particularly the battles, politics, and personalities of the Civil War. I chose sources that largely feature the stories of African Americans, in order to bring to life the aspirations, courage, fears, and sorrows of black people living through this period. Their experiences are placed in the context of major national events affecting black Americans, such as the rise of the domestic slave trade, the Fugitive Slave Laws, the Emancipation Proclamation, and the Republican Congress's Reconstruction policies. But this is a book for everyone, from any background. African American history is American history. The insights here are the insights from which every American can gain and grow.

The illustrations in *Traveling the Freedom Road*, wherever possible, also show young people in contemporary prints, drawings, daguerreotypes, and photographs. All the images are archival, and all are held in the Prints and Photographs, Rare Books and Special Collections, Manuscript, or Geography and Maps Divisions of the Library of Congress. Called "the Nation's Memory," the Library has an unparalleled collection of Civil War materials, as well as written, visual, recorded, and digital items that chronicle the origins and development of the United States.

I was excited to use the Library's collections and humbled by the stories I discovered. The words of ordinary people illuminating days and years of harshness and cruelty, resilience and strength, and pride and hope, are profoundly moving. Young readers and old, children and parents, and teachers and students can share them together, embracing a history that not only shaped the nineteenth century, but continues to inspire us today.

Slaves of the Rebel Gen.¹ Thomas F. Drayton.
Hilton Head
S.C.

During the Civil War, the North (Union) and South (Confederacy) fought to determine whether slavery would continue in the United States. In this photograph, taken in May 1862, slaves in Hilton Head, South Carolina, pose with a Union soldier (front, left) after Union forces reclaimed this part of South Carolina from the Confederacy. The slaves' owner, Thomas F. Drayton, was a general in the Confederate army.

INTRODUCTION

COUNTRIES HAVE STORIES TO TELL, JUST AS PEOPLE DO. What happened in the United States ten or fifty or a hundred years ago—what Americans believed, what they saw, what they felt, how they acted—shows us why or how we became the way we are today. What we call history is not just about the past. History moves with us. We carry it wherever we go, a backpack full of questions, ideas, surprises, mistakes, victories, explanations, and, sometimes, answers. History is always ready to reveal something about ourselves if we just look and ask.

The Civil War ended more than 140 years ago, but the legacy of slavery, the divisions between African Americans and white Americans, the persistence of racial discrimination, and even racial violence are, sadly, still a part of our lives. But so, too, are the efforts of both black and white people to overcome racism, to correct injustice, to fight for equality. We can take from our country's story signs and examples of courage and hope.

Traveling the Freedom Road actually tells two stories. It recounts the experiences of African Americans—slave and free; children, teenagers, and men and women; ordinary and extraordinary—who lived through the time of slavery, the Civil War, and the period known as Reconstruction, when the North and South tried to become one country again. It shows African Americans surviving hardships, fighting for liberty, and believing in a better future—a future when one's whole life was not decided by the color of one's skin.

This book also describes what was happening in the United States and the state governments during these times: what laws were made, what the political leaders did and felt, and what major events took place. It considers how happenings in the wider world were reflected in the everyday lives of African Americans. They might not have known the words of the U.S. Constitution, the Missouri Compromise, or the Fugitive Slave Law, but nineteenth-century black Americans knew what it was like to be enslaved. Their struggles, sufferings, and triumphs, their resistance and their spirit all played a huge part in our country's story.

Racism and slavery divided Americans and challenged our beliefs even before the United States was born. The story goes back to 1619, when the first Africans are known to have arrived in what would become our country. They landed in the colony of Virginia, and they were not slaves. They became "indentured servants," men, women, and children who worked without pay for a family or business, as the people they worked for had paid for their passage across the Atlantic. However, the servants worked for only a set period of time, after which they were free. White Europeans became indentured servants, too. But over time and as laws changed in the colonies, white servants always gained their liberty eventually, but black servants were bound to a master for life. Black people were identified with being enslaved; white people were not.

UNITED STATES SLAVE TRADE.

The slave trade was a brutal business. Women, men, and children were brought from Africa to be sold in the United States. African Americans, who were born in the United States, were also sold. In this print, a mother and two children look on at two slave traders who are selling them and the men shown here in chains.

How could one person own another? Why would he or she want to? In fact, people had been enslaved for thousands of years before the United States was founded. Slavery had been common in Europe, Africa, and Asia. After a war, the defeated people were often made to serve as slaves. African slaves, carried in European ships, were taken to Latin America and the Caribbean as early as the 1500s. The Europeans who settled what would become the United States knew slavery existed. They had plenty of space and land but needed workers. Slavery provided cheap labor, especially for planting and harvesting crops on the large plantations of the South. Since slaves were property, like horses or beds or blankets, an owner could also make money by selling them to another person. Because slaves from Africa looked different—had a different skin color—and because their way of life and customs were also different, supporters of slavery could convince themselves that Africans and their descendants were not equal, that they were even less than human, and it was right that they should be enslaved.

At the same time that slavery existed, many white Americans prized the idea of freedom. When, in the 1770s, the thirteen colonies wanted their liberty from British rule, representatives from each colony gathered and wrote the Declaration of Independence, which stated certain rights:

> **We hold these truths to be self-evident, that all men are created equal, that they are endowed by their Creator with certain unalienable Rights, that among these are Life, Liberty, and the pursuit of Happiness.**

"*All* men are created equal," not just white men; liberty is a *right*. These are the words of the founders of the United States. The founders were telling the world that their country would be a place where every person, no matter where he or she came from, would be free. Yet some of the men who signed the Declaration of Independence, including Thomas Jefferson, the third U.S. president, owned slaves. Remember, slaves were property—abolishing (doing away with) slavery would take away much of their owners' wealth as well as their workers. So those who owned slaves and those who thought enslaving people was wrong reached a compromise. They accepted enslavement of Africans in the United States, even though allowing slavery was a contradiction of the Declaration's words.

African Americans were aware of this contradiction. They pointed it out whenever they could in the fight for freedom. "See your declaration, Americans!! Do you understand your own language?" black American David Walker wrote in frustration in 1829. He was so outraged by the cruelties of slavery, he called for a violent revolution to end it. But it was civil war, not revolution, that finally ended slavery. As the Civil War president Abraham Lincoln said, "A house divided against itself cannot stand."

In this book you will read about a country that was divided. During the 1800s, as the United States grew westward, there were more and more Americans on each side of the slavery question: those who were for it and those who were against it. But you will also read about the people who never lost sight of the goal: liberty, unity, dignity for everyone. Travel the freedom road with them as they make their own history and tell their own stories.

Thomas Jefferson, a slave owner and future president of the United States, wrote this draft of the Declaration of Independence in June 1776. He made changes and corrections right on the page.

Mary and Emily Edmonson (from left) were teenagers when they tried to escape slavery aboard a boat headed

SLAVERY

ON THE NIGHT OF APRIL 15, 1848, THIRTEEN-YEAR-OLD Emily Edmonson, her fifteen-year-old sister, Mary, and four of their brothers secretly boarded a schooner named *Pearl* docked at a wharf on the Potomac River in Washington, D.C. Though their father was a free man, the six siblings were slaves because their mother was enslaved. According to the laws of Washington, D.C., and many states, children born to an enslaved mother were also slaves.

The Edmonson children had good jobs in the capital city, but their wages were not their own—what they earned belonged to their masters. They were well treated, but they were not at liberty to live where they wanted to, or to work at what they chose. And what they chose that rainy night in April was freedom. The plan was for the *Pearl* to sail down the Potomac, then up the Chesapeake Bay to a place where the seventy-seven slaves aboard would be picked up to then travel by land to the free-state city of Philadelphia, Pennsylvania.

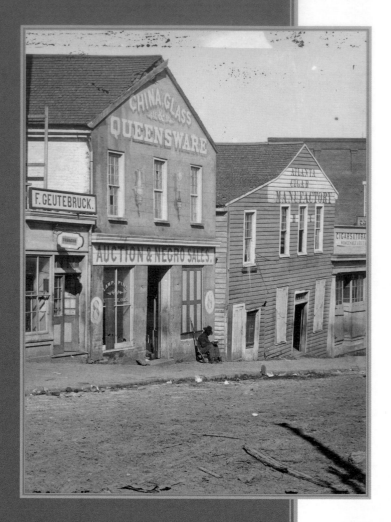

Slave traders often brought enslaved men, women, and children to a central location— such as this building that advertised "Auction & Negro Sales"—to be sold at auction. This auction house, photographed in 1864, was located on Whitehall Street in Atlanta, Georgia.

The Edmonson girls hid in the schooner's hold with the others. They knew the risk they were taking. If they were caught trying to escape, they would likely be sold to a slave trader. They would be forced to leave their D.C. home and would be taken farther south, where the chances of escape diminished with each mile. The Edmonson sisters might never work as household servants again. Instead, they might toil endlessly in the hot cotton fields of the Southern states. Like many other enslaved people who had been sold at the whim of an owner, they might never see their parents or their other brothers and sisters again.

This is what did—and did not— happen to Emily, Mary, and their brothers. Before it reached the Chesapeake, the *Pearl* was captured by those who enforced the slave laws. A slave trader bought them all and took the siblings to New Orleans. There they would have stayed, except that a yellow fever epidemic broke out in the city. To make sure the sisters did not catch the disease and die—leaving the trader without profitable young and pretty female slaves to sell—they were sent north to Virginia, while their brothers remained in Louisiana. In the meantime, their father, Paul Edmonson, had been trying to find a way to purchase their freedom. He met the minister Henry Ward Beecher, a white man, who had a church in Brooklyn, New York. They raised enough money to buy the Edmonson sisters and set them free. Eventually, two of their brothers were freed as well. A third, sold to a new owner, successfully escaped in 1859.

Emily and Mary were sent to school in Cortland, New York, and then to Oberlin, Ohio. The sisters began to speak out against slavery. They became abolitionists—people who demanded that slavery become illegal everywhere in the United States. Mary died from tuberculosis at a young age, but Emily lived to teach at a school for young African American women in Washington, D.C., and to marry, have children, and raise them as free Americans. She also lived to see the Thirteenth Amendment to the United States Constitution passed by Congress and ratified by most states in 1865, forever ending slavery in this country.

Why did the Constitution, the basic rules that govern the United States, allow slavery in the first place? Like the signers of the Declaration of Independence, some of the men who wrote the Constitution in 1787 lived in the Southern states and owned slaves. These drafters of the Constitution were convinced that they could not afford to grow and harvest crops without slave labor. In the 1700s, people had also owned slaves in the North, but in the Northern states, slavery eventually died out. It was less practical and not as affordable to have slaves work in the small shops and businesses and on the farms of the North as it was on large Southern plantations.

Vermont's constitution was the first in the North to ban slavery. In 1777, it stated:

> [N]o male person, born in this country, or brought from over sea, ought to be holden by law, to serve any person, as a servant, slave or apprentice, after he arrives to the age of twenty-one Years, nor female, in like manner, after she arrives to the age of eighteen years, unless they are bound by their own consent . . .

Vermont's law went much further than the U.S. Constitution would. Although it was intended to "secure the blessings of liberty" to Americans and their children, the U.S. Constitution, passed in 1787, never said that slavery was wrong. The best it did was to give future lawmakers the power to ban the international slave trade—the business of bringing slaves from Africa. But this did not occur until 1808, which allowed slave traders and owners twenty-one more years to increase the number of Africans enslaved in this country—twenty-one more years to force tens of thousands more people to leave their homes, to pack them into crowded ships to cross the Atlantic, and to sell them on auction blocks.

The slave trade was cruel and brutal. Imagine being kidnapped from your home and family and brought to a different country, never to return again. Olaudah Equiano was born in Guinea, in the western part of Africa. When Equiano was eleven, "one day, when all our people were gone out to their works as usual, and only I and my dear sister were left to mind the house, two men and a woman got over our walls, and in a moment seized us both, . . . stopped our mouths, and ran off with us into the nearest wood." He was soon separated from his sister and worked as a slave in several African households, before he endured the horrors of a slave ship sailing to America—chains,

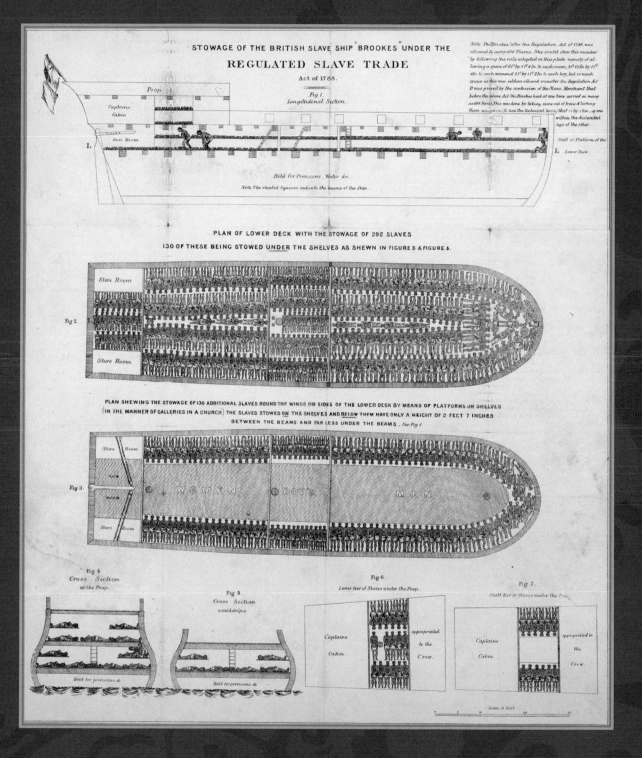

Ships bringing slaves from Africa crowded in as many people as they could for the crossing over the Atlantic Ocean. These plans for the British slave ship Brookes, *drawn in 1788, show how 292 slaves could be made to fit lying crammed next to each other, side by side.*

filth, illness, whippings, and for some aboard, death. He eventually arrived in Virginia and was later sent to England. Equiano published his life story in 1789.

Just two years before Equiano's book appeared, white Americans had written the Constitution and accepted it as the law of the land in 1787. In another concession to slavery, the Constitution stated in a clause that a slave who ran away from his owner—a fugitive slave—could not be freed even if he or she reached a free state. According to this clause, Emily and Mary Edmonson would have remained slaves, even if they had reached Philadelphia. What's more, they would have had to be returned to their

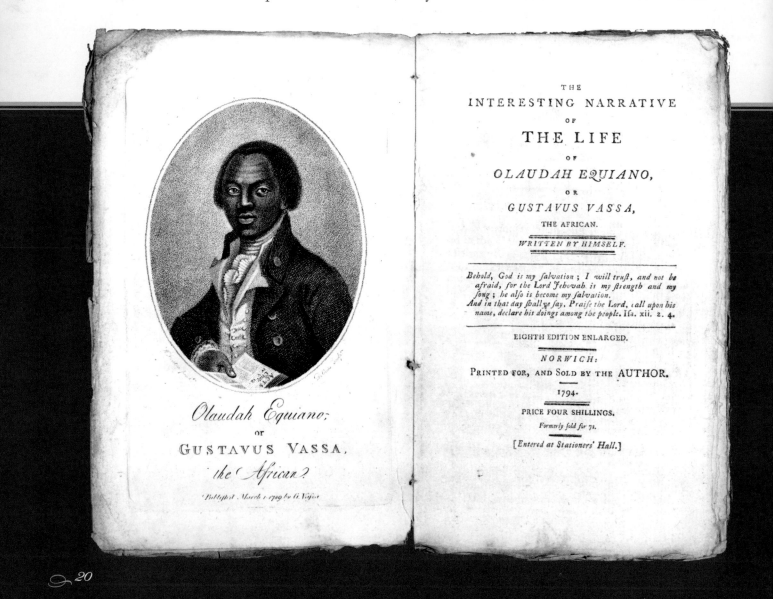

owner. The Fugitive Slave Clause, as it was called, was unpopular in the free states of the North, which did not want to act as police for the slave states or send anyone back into slavery.

For a while it appeared that slavery might gradually end in the South on its own. Before 1800, many of those enslaved worked in the tobacco fields of Virginia, Maryland, and Delaware. The land was overused and was damaged during fighting in the American Revolution; fewer plants grew, and tobacco farming brought in less money. Some masters began to free their slaves so that they would not have to pay to clothe and feed them; others did so because they came to believe that the liberty promised by the Declaration of Independence was for all.

Then one invention changed everything. Eli Whitney designed and built a cotton gin in 1793. Now planters could make a huge profit by growing and selling what was known as "short staple" cotton. The gin quickly separated the seeds of this plant from the fibers used to make cloth. It had once taken a person working by hand a day to clean a pound of cotton, but with a gin, he or she could clean fifty pounds. Cotton planted in the lower South—Georgia, Alabama, Mississippi, and Louisiana—could make a man or woman rich. But who

IN THE COTTON FIELD.

ABOVE *This card, printed circa 1863, shows slaves picking cotton. The growing of cotton used the labor of thousands upon thousands of enslaved people.*

OPPOSITE *This copy of Olaudah Equiano's life story was printed in 1794, five years after he published the first edition. The book was a best seller in its time; this was the eighth time it was printed. Gustavus Vassa was a name given to Equiano by one of his owners, before he achieved his freedom.*

would sow, harvest, and process the plant? Thousands upon thousands of slaves. A Virginia planter who once grew tobacco could make much more money by selling his slaves to work in the cotton fields than by freeing them. After 1808, domestic slaves—slaves born in the United States—became even more valuable because new slaves could no longer be brought from Africa.

Buying and selling people for profit was an ugly business, with men, women, and children treated harshly and handled and displayed like animals. "I remember a man named Rough something or other who bought forty or fifty slaves at the time and carried them to Richmond to resell," said Cornelia Andrews of North Carolina, who was sold to a new owner as a child. "He had four big black horses hooked to a cart, and behind this cart he chained the slaves, and they had to walk, or trot all the way to Richmond. The little ones Mr. Rough would throw up in the cart and off they'd go. . . . They say that there was one day at Smithfield that three hundred slaves were sold on the block. . . . People came from far and near, even from New Orleans to those slave sales." Sold to a third master, Cornelia Andrews was "whipped in public . . . for breaking dishes and being slow." At age eighty-seven, she still bore the scars.

In the first half of the nineteenth century, the domestic slave trade flourished, as more and more slaves were needed to work on cotton and other plantations. These plantations were springing up farther and farther west. The United States was growing. In 1803, the government bought from France the Louisiana Purchase, a large stretch of land that expanded U.S. borders beyond the Mississippi River. New settlers came to this territory, some with their slaves, some who opposed slavery. Expanding settlement raised the issue of slavery again. Should slavery exist in the states that were forming from this territory, which reached from the Mississippi to the Rocky Mountains? Should slavery spread with the growth of the country? Slave states said yes—they were afraid that slavery would be abolished if too many free states joined the Union

LEFT *Enslaved people usually lived in simple, small, crude dwellings, unlike this plantation house in Mount Airy, Louisiana, where wealthy owners lived.*

OPPOSITE *At slave auctions like this one in the South, buyers could inspect the children, men, and women being sold and bid for the ones they wanted. The number of auctions selling slaves born in the United States increased after slaves could no longer be brought from Africa.*

and voted against it. Free states worried that if slavery was allowed to spread, it would take away the jobs of paid white workers moving to those states. Many could see that slavery was simply wrong: inhuman, unjust, and completely at odds with the spirit of the country. Others thought it was more important to keep all the states together in one union even if they had to accept slavery to appease the South.

The first crisis came in 1820, when Missouri wanted to enter the Union as a slave state. In order to keep the number of slave and free states even, Congress reached the Missouri Compromise: Missouri became a slave state, but Maine, in the Northeast, was admitted as a free state. Slavery was banned in the northern part of the Louisiana Purchase. Americans were coming to accept a dividing line between the free North and the slave South. The feelings of Americans on both sides would become stronger as time went by. Both sides would try to influence Congress. But Congress made its deals and passed its laws with no advice from the enslaved. Yet its decision to allow the growth of slavery according to the Missouri Compromise affected every single slave who lived through the toil, hardship, and tragedy of being owned by someone else.

What Was Slavery Like?

"Come daybreak you hear the guinea fowls . . . and the roosters . . . then purty soon the wind rises a little, and you can hear an old bell donging away on some plantation a mile or two off, and then more bells at other places and maybe a horn, and purty soon yonder goes old Master's old ram horn with a long toot and then some short toots, and here comes the overseer down the row of cabins, hollering right and left. . . . Bells and horns! Bells for this and horns for that! All we knew was [to] go and come by the bells and horns!"

Slaves didn't just plant and pick cotton—they did all the work on a plantation, in the fields and inside the house. Here they use a cotton gin to separate the seeds of the plant from its fibers. The enslaved man on the left is smiling. It was common for white artists to portray slaves as easygoing and contented, rather than show the harshness of their lives.

This was what Charley Williams remembered about waking up when he was an enslaved child in Louisiana. Work, work, work. Every minute there was work to do and there were rules to follow. A slave could not sleep late or take his time eating breakfast or stop for a break when the sun beat down on the fields. His life was not his own. Many slaves were forced to work so hard that they were almost always exhausted; there was little rest during the endless days.

James Abbot was an enslaved child in Missouri. If Missouri had become a free state, James might have gone to school, done chores for his parents, and played with other kids. Instead, he worked from sunrise to sunset and beyond. His master was sick and "lay from the opening o' spring, 'bout the time flies come, 'til wheat-sowing time in the fall. . . . All that time he made me stand [at the] side o' his bed—keepin' the flies off him. I was just seven years old but there I had to stand, day and night, night and day. Course I'd sleep sometimes when he was sleepin'. Sometimes when I'd doze, my brush would fall on his face. Then he'd take his stick and whack me a few across the head and he'd say, 'Now I dare you to cry.'"

Although some owners did not beat their slaves, violence was a part of everyday life for most. If a slave seemed slow or disobedient, he or she would often be hit or whipped, even if too sick or hungry or tired to complete a task. Slaves were punished for not doing exactly as they were told. Harriet Tubman, who guided more than two hundred slaves to freedom between 1849 and 1860, was an enslaved teenager when she refused to tie down another slave so he could be beaten. The overseer—the man who managed the slaves for the owner—hit her in the head with a heavy weight. The blow caused her to suffer from bouts of unconsciousness for the rest of her life.

"Lord! I've seen such brutish doings—running [slaves] with hounds and whipping them till they were bloody," recounted Lucretia Alexander, who was a twelve-year-old slave when the Civil War started. "I remember one time they caught a man named George Tinsley. They put the dogs on him and they bit him and tore all his clothes off. . . . Then they put him in the stocks. The stocks were a big piece of timber with hinges in it. . . . They would lift it up and put your head in it. There were holes for your head, hands and feet. . . . Then they would shut it up and they would lay the whip on you and you couldn't do anything but wiggle and holler." David

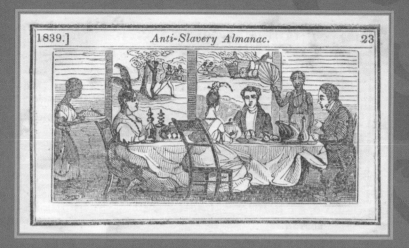

ABOVE *A young slave serves dinner while another fans the white people at the table to keep them cool, in this page from an 1839 anti-slavery book.*

RIGHT *Harriet Tubman was enslaved in Dorchester County, Maryland, for almost thirty years. Afraid she would be sold when her master died, she fled to Philadelphia in 1849, but she returned to the South many times to help other slaves escape.*

THE LASH.

Whipping was a common punishment for slaves who tried to escape, but an owner or overseer (a person who supervised work) could also whip enslaved people who seemed to be working too slowly or who showed too much independence. This card was one of a series about slave life published in 1863.

Blont, enslaved in North Carolina, saw an "overseer beat some of the half grown boys till the blood ran down to their heels."

Fear kept most slaves in line—fear of pain, fear of permanent injury, fear of death. Slaves were whipped until they bled and sometimes beaten until they died. Owners had the right, under the laws and codes of the slave states—and through custom—to treat slaves in any way they chose. Slaves had no rights—after all, they weren't considered to be people, but property. They were forbidden to leave their homes without permission, and if they were caught without a pass from the owner, they would be whipped. They could not legally marry, and they often lived separated from other family members.

Owners decided what and how much food slaves would eat and what clothes they would wear. By keeping their slaves afraid, undernourished, and poorly clothed, slave owners were better able to control them. A tired, weak, and cold slave was less likely to cause problems or try to escape. Charles Crawley of Virginia was one of many who had no shoes in the winter. "I 'member one time the snow was a foot deep and I had to gather the corn," he recalled. "I was barefooted and barehanded. My feet hurt so bad and my hands got so stiff I couldn't work my fingers. . . . That night my feet cracked open and next morning when I had to make the fires I left a track o' blood across the floor."

But the cruelest thing about slavery was that the owner tried to control not only a slave's body, but his or her heart and mind as well. Slavery encouraged ignorance. In every Southern state, slaves were forbidden to learn to read and write. Owners feared that writing and reading would open up a whole new world to enslaved people. It would help them to understand what was wrong about slavery, give them ideas for how they might better themselves, and enable them to write letters to other slaves and to abolitionists for support and help. Although a slave caught trying to learn was severely punished, some slaves thought it was so important to read and write that they taught themselves secretly or found a kind white person to teach them. Frederick Douglass, who escaped slavery to become a great abolitionist, wrote of his childhood in Baltimore, Maryland: "[My] lessons in reading were learned from little school boys in the street and out of the way places where [I] could not be observed or interfered with. In fact, the street became [my] school and the pavements and fences in [my] neighborhood became [my] blackboard."

Frederick Douglass, who escaped from slavery when he was a young man, wrote several full-length books about his life. At the bottom of this manuscript page, he writes that the "street became his school and the pavements . . . his blackboard." Douglass composed this piece for an article about him in the National Cyclopaedia of American Biography.

THE PARTING "Buy us too".

In every way, slavery tried to take away the dignity and self-respect of the enslaved. The threat of punishment was always present, and, perhaps greater, so was the threat of separation. Mothers, fathers, and children were frequently sold to different masters, forced to live apart from each other for the rest of their lives. If a slave showed too much independence or had a strong will, or had tried to escape and was caught, he or she would often be sold to a buyer farther south. It was much harder to flee north from Louisiana or Alabama than it was from Maryland or Virginia.

Sometimes owners sold their slaves to make money. Selling a young slave brought in profit, and from the buyer's point of view, purchasing a child was a good investment—he or she would work when young, and work even more as an adult. "Babies were snatched from their mothers . . . and sold to speculators. Children were separated from sisters an' brothers and never saw each other again," said Delia Garlic, who was enslaved from birth. "Course they cried; you think they [would] not cry when they were sold like cattle? I could tell you 'bout it all day, but even then you couldn't guess the awfulness of it. It's bad to belong to folks that own you soul and body."

Henry Bibb, who was born a slave in Kentucky in 1815, wrote: "I was taken away from my mother, and hired out to labor for various persons, eight or ten years in succession, and all my wages were expended for the education of Harriet White, my playmate." Henry and Harriet were both just children when Harriet's father had given Henry to her as a present, to be her slave. "It was then my sorrows and sufferings commenced," remembered Henry. "It was then I first commenced seeing and feeling that I was a wretched slave, compelled to work under the lash without wages, and often without clothes enough to hide my nakedness. I have often worked without half to eat, both late and early, by day and by night." Henry suffered without his family to comfort him, while Harriet was loved, pampered, well clothed, and well fed.

ABOVE *Sometimes slave owners gave their children, grandchildren, or nieces and nephews a young slave to be their companion and work for them as they grew up. But white and African American children also played together, like those in this picture, before custom and experience taught them how different and separate their lives would be as adults.*

OPPOSITE LEFT *Printed in 1863, this card shows the pain and sadness a woman feels when her family is forcefully separated. Their little child reaches after his father.*

OPPOSITE RIGHT *Not only enslaved adults but also children were sold away from their families. This illustration, in which a character named Little Lewis is taken away from his brother and friends, originally appeared in a story in* The Child's Anti-Slavery Book, *written by abolitionists for young people, published in 1859.*

How could slaveholders justify this treatment of human beings? The supporters of slavery thought that black people were less than human. Slavery, they said, was a way to help these people, who on their own could not work hard or take care of themselves. They were simple and childlike and needed to be protected. As slaves, they were provided with food, clothes, and a place to live. They were also taught the Christian religion, which white people considered to be superior to any African religion. The enslaved attended church—usually segregated from white worshipers—where white ministers told them it was a virtue to obey one's master. Even those slaves who were treated relatively well lacked what they wanted most: respect, equality, and independence.

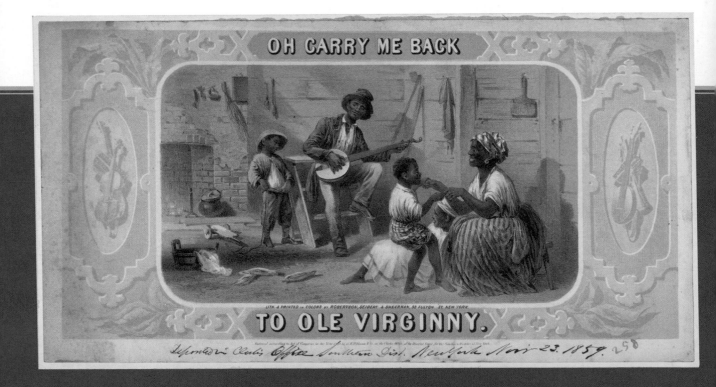

Slave owners argued that slaves were better off in the care of white people than they would be on their own. Pictures drawn by whites in the 1800s, like this 1859 label from a tobacco package, often showed what whites wanted to believe: that African Americans were happy, carefree, and living together in harmony—which was far from the reality of an enslaved person's life.

Slaves who tried to escape risked pursuit by dogs and men armed with guns. They could be captured and whipped or sold to an owner far away from their families and friends. It took great determination and courage to overcome the fear of capture.

Free but Not Equal

History often links black Americans and slavery, but, in fact, not all African Americans were slaves. Some Africans came to this country as free men and women. Some slaves earned money by being hired out. Unlike Henry Bibb, they were allowed to keep it, and they used their earnings to buy their freedom and, if they could, their families' freedom, too. Others were freed by their masters. Freedom was granted to those who fought as soldiers in the Revolutionary War, and slaves in the Northern states were freed by law. Free black women gave birth to free children—children who never had to live as slaves.

Some African Americans gained their freedom by running away from their owners. Those who tried to escape to freedom were in constant danger. After leaving the plantation where she was enslaved, Harriet Jacobs's first step was to hide in the house of a friend, not far from where she had run away. After "a week had passed in terrible suspense, [my] pursuers came into such close vicinity that I concluded they had tracked me to my hiding-place. I flew out of the house, and concealed myself in a thicket of bushes. There I remained in an agony of fear. . . . Suddenly, a reptile of some kind seized my leg. In my fright, I struck a blow which loosened its hold, but I could not see what it was; I only knew it was something cold and slimy. The pain I felt soon indicated that the bite was poisonous."

Amazingly, Jacobs then hid in a tiny space above a storeroom in her grandmother's house for seven years. The ceiling was too low for her to stand up. "The rats and mice ran over my bed," she later wrote. "It seemed horrible to sit or lie in a cramped position day after day, without one gleam of light. . . . [F]or weeks I was tormented by hundreds of little red insects, fine as a needle's point, that pierced through my skin, and produced an intolerable burning." Yet Jacobs preferred all her suffering to being a slave. Eventually she did escape to New York, and her employer there purchased her freedom.

Henry Box Brown was another slave who escaped in a particularly imaginative way. He had himself shipped via Adams Express, a freight service, from Richmond, Virginia, to Philadelphia. Brown paid forty dollars for someone to box him in a crate three feet long by two and a half feet deep by two feet wide. He made it to safety and was helped by the Pennsylvania Anti-Slavery Society. The box that Brown escaped in became a symbol in the abolitionist movement, showing the inhumane confinement of slavery. It was said that when Brown climbed out of the box, he sang a song of thanksgiving.

By 1860, 488,000 free blacks like Harriet Jacobs and Henry Box Brown lived in the United States. Those who lived in the South needed to carry papers that proved they were free. Often, they were not allowed to be out at night. In many states, free blacks had to register with the local police or courts so that whites would know where they lived. They were not served at restaurants or hotels and had to sit

Henry Box Brown emerges from the box he had himself shipped in to escape slavery. In this print, fugitive slave and abolitionist Frederick Douglass (second from left) is one of the well-wishers who looks on. Brown published a book about his imaginative but difficult escape in 1849.

in the balcony at theaters. Most worked as contract laborers on plantations, usually with almost the same restrictions as slaves. Aaron Griggs of Louisiana agreed "to go out to the fields at the same hours with the people of the plantation & to work with the plantation overseer." He could not leave for another job until he completed his contract.

Some Southern free blacks worked as barbers, carpenters, blacksmiths, or tailors; others filled unskilled jobs at tobacco and iron factories. Especially in the cities of Charleston, South Carolina, and New Orleans, Louisiana, a number of free blacks became educated and prosperous, some even owning slaves themselves. Sometimes, these slaves would actually be family members, "bought" so that husband and wife or father and child could be reunited. But most often, free blacks owned slaves for the reason whites did: as a source of cheap labor. William Ellison of South Carolina was a successful manufacturer of cotton gins who paid for the freedom of his wife and daughter. As a mark of his acceptance in the community, he was allowed to sit with the white worshipers in his church, instead of with the slaves and free blacks in the balcony. Ellison was likely the son of a white owner—children of enslaved women and white men were sometimes freed by their fathers. Yet as a black man, he could not be assured of continued good treatment, especially as the tensions between slave and free states grew.

In the North, free blacks had fewer restrictions than in the South, although in what were then the Northwestern states (Illinois, Indiana, Michigan, Ohio, and Wisconsin), where whites felt particularly threatened by black competition for jobs, codes often insisted that African Americans register at local government offices. Indiana, Illinois, and eventually Iowa and Oregon barred free blacks from settling altogether. Even in Northeastern states, freedom did not protect African Americans from racial discrimination. In many cases, they could not travel on public transportation, such as streetcars, or go to restaurants, theaters, or hotels—or, if they could, they were seated separately from white people. Some schools were integrated, but in the big cities in New York, New Jersey, Pennsylvania, and Ohio, where many blacks lived, schools were segregated. Black Americans could not vote or serve on juries, except in Massachusetts. Many found jobs hard to get, since white workers objected to working alongside them. Other jobs were not open to them at all. In 1825, Congress even passed a law that forbade African Americans from delivering the mail.

However, free blacks could legally marry. They formed their own churches and aid societies and could begin to build their own businesses and communities. Some achieved commercial success, like James Forten of Philadelphia. Born a free black in 1766, Forten voluntarily served in the Revolutionary War because he believed in equality and independence. He had an enormously successful business as a sailmaker and became, unlike most free blacks, wealthy. He was also a well-known abolitionist, speaking and writing in behalf of liberty for the enslaved.

STATE OF VIRGINIA,
City of Petersburg, to wit: No. 2921.

Harriet Bolling ⸻ a free *woman* of color, who was heretofore registered in the Clerk's Office of the Hustings Court of the said ~~Town~~ City, this day delivered up to me, the former certificate of *her* registration, and applied for a renewal of the same, which is granted *her*; and *she* is now of the following discription, to wit: *four* feet *9½* inches high, about *forty two* years of age, of a *mulatto* complexion, has *some small dark spots or splotches on each of her cheeks, a scar on her left wrist occasioned by a cut; and was emancipated in this Court by James Bolling by deed dated 14 May 1842, and has been permitted by the Court to remain in this Commonwealth and reside in Petersburg. This renewal is granted her by an order of the Court of the 17th of October 1850.*

In Testimony whereof, I, DAVID M. BERNARD, Clerk of the said Hustings Court, have hereto set my hand and affixed the Seal of the said court, this *11* day of *June* A. D., 185*1*.

D. M. Bernard Clk

John Dodson Mayor

Charlotte Forten, James's granddaughter, was sent to live in Salem, Massachusetts, when she was sixteen, and there she studied in a public school that accepted her as a black student. She described her days in the diary she kept. "How bright and beautiful are these May mornings!" she wrote in 1854. "The air is so pure and balmy, the trees are in full blossom, and the little birds sing sweetly. I stand by the window listening to their music, but suddenly remember that I have an Arithmetic lesson which employes me until breakfast; then to school, recited my lessons. . . . After dinner practised a music lesson, did some sewing, and then took a pleasant walk by the water." But Charlotte also grew up as an abolitionist, and wrote a few days later, "How strange it is that in a world so beautiful, there can be so much wickedness . . . while many are enjoying themselves in their happy homes . . . millions . . . are suffering in chains."

Abolitionists opened the New-York African Free-Schools in 1787. This engraving, taken from a drawing by a thirteen-year-old student, shows Free-School No. 2. Among the most valuable lessons the students learned was the importance of freedom.

[1839.]   Anti-Slavery Almanac.   13

COLORED SCHOLARS EXCLUDED FROM SCHOOLS.

This illustration from the Anti-Slavery Almanac, *published by Northern abolitionists in 1839, shows a free African American mother and two children being turned away from a whites-only school. Even in the North, prejudice kept most schools from being integrated.*

Although most Northern schools were not integrated, free black children in the North could still learn to read and write. One group of schools that taught them was the New-York African Free-Schools, founded by abolitionists. Even these schools had their enemies. Charles Andrews wrote in 1830 that a school such as these "was far from being a popular one; the prejudice of a large portion of the community were against it." Nevertheless, black children were taught "reading, writing, arithmetic, geography, English grammar, navigation and astronomy," and practical skills. In 1830, there were 154 girls in the sewing department, "of which number there are, acquainted with making garments and marking, 56; capable of knitting stockings, socks, suspenders &c. 42."

African American students not only learned their subjects, they learned to express their hatred of slavery. Thomas Sidney, a twelve-year-old, wrote this poem, "On Freedom":

> Freedom will break the tyrant's chain,
> And shatter all his whole domain;
> From slavery she will always free,
> And all her aim is liberty.

Restrictions and discrimination did not kill the spirit of free black children or indeed of most free black Americans. Nor did free blacks forget the plight of their enslaved brothers and sisters. They believed that the United States should live up to its promise of freedom for everyone. There were white Americans who agreed. They fought for a legal end to slavery, and their voices grew louder and more urgent as the decades of the nineteenth century passed.

RIGHT *These flowers were drawn by Eveleen Simmons, a student at the Myrtilla Miner School for Free Colored Girls in Washington, D.C., in the 1850s. People in Washington, D.C., could legally own slaves. Many whites objected to black children receiving an education even in segregated schools.*

OPPOSITE The Child's Anti-Slavery Book, *published in 1859 by the Sunday-School Union in New York, contained four stories about the harsh life enslaved children suffered. It opens with a moving appeal to white children: "Are all the children in America free like you? . . . Though born beneath the same sun and on the same soil . . . they are nevertheless SLAVES. Alas for them!"*

Eveleen Simmons, Jan 1854

A Is for Abolitionist

As the number of slaves continued to grow, there was also an ever-growing number of Americans who believed that no matter how kind or generous an owner might be, slavery was just plain wrong. These abolitionists wanted to abolish slavery. Many of them were against slavery for religious reasons. They thought that buying, selling, and owning a person went against the teachings of Christianity, which called on Christians to love all people and treat them fairly. *The Child's Anti-Slavery Book*, published in 1859, made the evils of slavery very clear:

Remember one great truth regarding slavery, namely, that a slave is a human being, held and used as property by another human being, and that *it is always* A SIN AGAINST GOD *to thus hold and use a human being as property!* . . . Yet that is what every slaveholder does. *He uses his slaves as property.* He reckons them as worth so many dollars. . . . He sells him, gives him away, uses his labor without paying him wages, claims his children as so many more dollars added to his estate, and when he dies wills him to his heirs forever.

THE CHILD'S

ANTI-SLAVERY BOOK:

CONTAINING A

Few Words about American Slave Children.

AND

STORIES OF SLAVE-LIFE.

1871

TEN ILLUSTRATIONS.

New-York:

PUBLISHED BY CARLTON & PORTER,
SUNDAY-SCHOOL UNION, 200 MULBERRY-STREET.

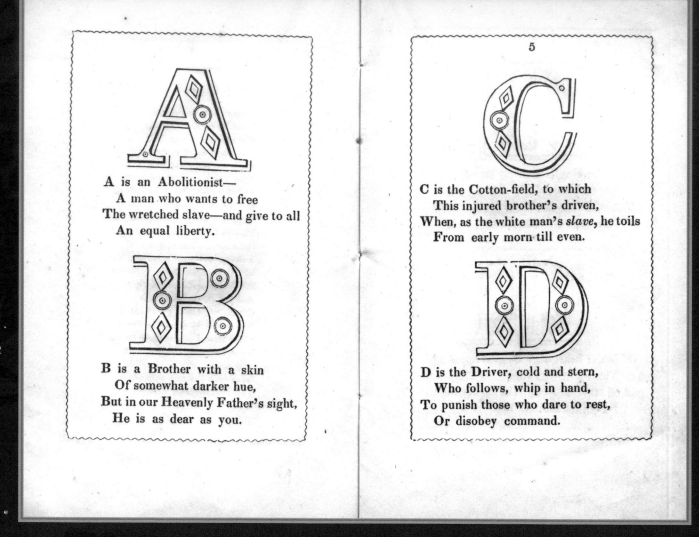

A is an Abolitionist—
A man who wants to free
The wretched slave—and give to all
An equal liberty.

B is a Brother with a skin
Of somewhat darker hue,
But in our Heavenly Father's sight,
He is as dear as you.

C is the Cotton-field, to which
This injured brother's driven,
When, as the white man's *slave*, he toils
From early morn till even.

D is the Driver, cold and stern,
Who follows, whip in hand,
To punish those who dare to rest,
Or disobey command.

This is the beginning of the Anti-Slavery Alphabet, *a book for children published in 1847. Although the rhymes are singsong and childlike, they describe the evils of slavery.*

At the end of the eighteenth century, Quakers, who had settled in America to find their own religious freedom, were among those who opposed slavery. Levi Coffin was a nineteenth-century Quaker and abolitionist—he and others ran the Underground Railroad, a system of escape routes, shelters, and sympathetic hosts who hid and fed runaway slaves as they headed from the South to the North. Other white people who played leading roles in the abolition movement included William Lloyd Garrison and Sarah and Angelina Grimké. Henry Highland Garnet, William Wells Brown, and Maria Stewart were black abolitionists. Runaway slaves also became abolitionists—perhaps the most famous were Harriet Tubman and Frederick Douglass. Tubman was so feared by slave owners that they offered $40,000 for her capture. Douglass published a well-known anti-slavery newspaper, the *North Star*, which later became *Frederick Douglass' Paper*.

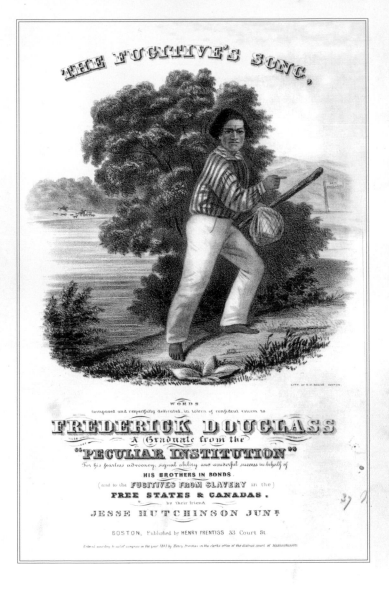

Frederick Douglass was one of many fugitive slaves who became abolitionists, writing and lecturing in the North on behalf of those still enslaved. Douglass was one of the most eloquent and powerful speakers, touching many people with his true story of hardship and triumph. This song was written in his honor.

FISH TOWN at BASSAU   LIBERIA

Black and white abolitionists did not always agree on the way to end slavery or how many rights black Americans should have. Sometimes they disagreed on whether blacks should live in the United States at all. Some whites did not support slavery, but they worried about the growing number of free blacks in the country. They did not believe that blacks and whites could—or should—live together peacefully, or as equals, in the United States. They thought that more owners would be willing to free their slaves if those newly freed agreed to settle in Africa. The American Colonization Society, founded in 1816, purchased land on Africa's west coast to form a new country, Liberia. The first group of free black colonists arrived there in 1822.

LEFT *Some African Americans immigrated to Liberia, on Africa's west coast, because they thought they could never be truly free and equal in the United States. This daguerreotype (an early kind of photograph) shows a Liberian woman from the McGill family in 1855, about thirty years after the first blacks emigrated.*

OPPOSITE *The American Colonization Society tried to persuade free African Americans that they would have a better life in Liberia, the country the society founded on Africa's west coast. Many society members were fearful that the presence of a large number of free blacks in the United States would lead to the end of slavery. This picture shows the shipping port of Bassau, Liberia.*

But the vast majority of free blacks in the United States did not want to emigrate. "The masses of the colored people, who *think* for themselves, have believed that the same effort made in working our way up in this country, and in civilizing the whites, would accomplish our object as certain and as easy as we could by emigrating to a foreign country," said John Rock, an African American lawyer and abolitionist. "This being our country, we have made up our minds to remain in it, and to try to make it worth living in."

In the 1850s and during the early part of the Civil War, some Americans again spoke out for colonization by African Americans—this time not in Africa but in Haiti and Central and South America. Again, some black Americans supported the idea, because they thought blacks could never be fairly treated or equal in the United States. But most were against it. "We are Americans, speaking the same language, adopting the

The large majority of free blacks, including those in this photograph taken sometime after 1860, did not travel to Liberia. This mother and child, attractive and well dressed, look very different from the way African Americans were often portrayed by artists of the time.

same customs, holding the same general opinions, . . . and shall rise or fall with Americans," wrote Frederick Douglass. "Upon the whole our history here has been one of progress and improvement, and in all the likelihoods of the case, will become more so."

When he said this in 1861, Douglass cast a positive light on the "progress" African Americans had made from the beginning of the nineteenth century. It is true that by the 1830s, black abolitionists and most white abolitionists had come to agree that their goal was to have all slaves freed immediately. They were also working together. The American Anti-Slavery Society, founded in 1833, was the first large organization to be started and directed by black as well as white Americans. By 1836 there were more than five hundred anti-slavery societies in the northern United States.

However, unlike most white abolitionists, black abolitionists worked not just to end slavery, but to gain racial equality, including the right to vote. They believed that being able to vote was *the only way to guarantee equality.* "Our work will not be done until the colored man is admitted as a full member in good and regular standing in the American body politic," argued Frederick Douglass. He attacked one of the arguments white people used to keep black men from voting: that African Americans knew nothing about politics. "It is said that the colored man is ignorant and therefore he shall not vote," continued Douglass. "In saying this, you lay down a rule for the black man that you apply to no other class of your citizens. I will hear nothing of . . . ignorance against the black man. . . . If he knows an honest man from a thief, he knows much more than some of our white voters." A group of African Americans in Kansas had the Declaration of Independence in mind when they wrote, "We contend that *our* right to vote is natural and inherent; resting upon the fact of our being born in this country, and upon the form of government under which we live."

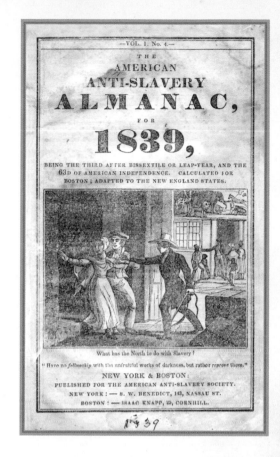

The American Anti-Slavery Almanac, *a yearly publication, was one of hundreds of books, pamphlets, and broadsides (posters) published by abolitionists to persuade people that slavery was wrong.*

    In the 1830s, many anti-slavery men and women began to think that it was not enough to convince people that enslaving a human being was morally wrong. They needed political power to elect a president who would oppose slavery, and congressmen who would pass the necessary laws to end it. A new organization, the American and Foreign Anti-Slavery Society, broke away from the American Anti-Slavery Society and was established in 1840. Its members were more politically active. They supported the newly formed Liberty Party, which ran anti-slavery candidates for public office. In the 1850s, the Republican Party would also form. Republicans were against spreading slavery to new territories and states, but they were willing to accept it in the states where it already existed. Still, the Republican Party was very unpopular in the South.

A Decade of Crisis

By 1850, some Americans were saying that there should be two countries—a free North and a slave South—but many people did not see this as a solution. In the 1850s, one big crisis after another pushed those who supported slavery and those who were against it further apart. First, the new territory the United States gained in the Mexican-American War (1846–1848) threatened to destroy the balance between the number of slave and free states. People living in California (part of this territory) wanted to make slavery illegal. Congress refused to accept California as a free state until its members passed several laws that became known as the Compromise of 1850. California would become a free state, but slavery would be allowed in the rest of the territory acquired from Mexico (Nevada, Utah, and parts of New Mexico, Colorado, and Arizona). Further, the slave trade would be abolished in Washington, D.C. Slaves could not be bought and sold in the city, but people would still be allowed to own slaves there.

Then, a new, stronger Fugitive Slave Law, part of the Compromise of 1850, required all states to assist in the return of runaway slaves to their owners, with strict enforcement. The only "proof" needed that a person declared a fugitive had escaped was an owner's testimony. Those accused could not speak on their own behalf. Federal commissioners received twice as much money when they decided in favor of the owner

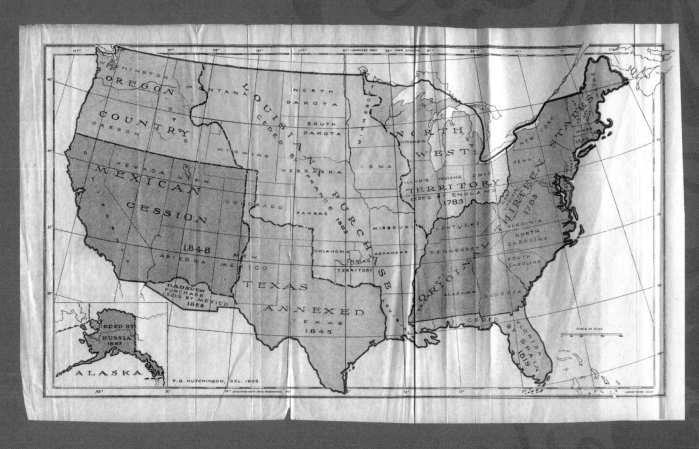

ABOVE *This 1903 map shows, in green (excluding Alaska), the territory ceded to the United States after the Mexican–American War. The earlier Louisiana Purchase (1803) is shown in gold. The area east of the Louisiana Purchase and north of Florida was all part of the United States by 1783.*

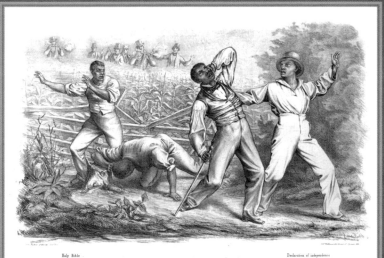

LEFT *This print shows the possible negative effects of the Fugitive Slave Law. Several white men in the upper left close in on four African American men, two of whom have been shot. The print makes it impossible to tell whether the black men are slaves or free. It does make clear that all African Americans were subject to suspicion and violence under the law. Words from the Declaration of Independence appear in the lower right.*

than they did if they found in favor of the person said to be a fugitive. If any ordinary citizen helped a runaway, she or he could be fined $1,000, go to jail for six months, or have to pay damages to the owner. Any U.S. official who did not enforce the law could also be fined $1,000 or the slave's entire value.

The North hated the law. Underground Railroad activities to assist runaways increased, rather than decreased. Before 1850, four free states had passed personal liberty laws, allowing an alleged slave a trial by jury and forbidding officials of state governments from aiding the federal government in the capture of escaped slaves. Between 1850 and 1860, ten free states passed new personal liberty laws or revised existing ones. These laws also fined or imprisoned anyone who tried to claim a free black as a slave. Southern states were upset by this resistance to the Fugitive Slave Law.

In 1854, the capture of the runaway Anthony Burns in Boston caused riots. Burns's story was national news. He had been enslaved in Virginia. From the age of seven, his owner, Charles Suttle, had sent him out to work for others. Year after year, Suttle kept the wages, giving Burns only 12½ cents every Christmas. When he was twenty, Burns escaped in a boat that took him to Boston. He arrived in February and had been there only three months when Suttle found him.

Under the law, the city was bound to return Burns, but there was a tremendous protest from both white and black Bostonians. One group attacked the courthouse to try to rescue Burns, and a policeman was killed. Another group raised the money to buy Burns's freedom, but the United States government would not allow this. On June 2, Burns was led to a boat bound for Virginia, while angry mobs crowded the path. It took the U.S. Army, Marines, and Coast Guard; a contingent of Massachusetts soldiers; and 1,500 men of the Boston Militia to guard Burns so the crowd could not rescue him.

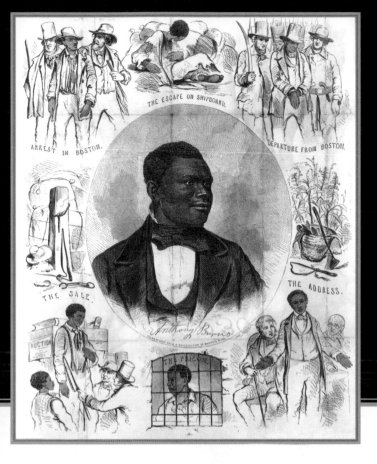

THE ESCAPE ON SHIPBOARD.

ARREST IN BOSTON.

DEPARTURE FROM BOSTON.

THE SALE.

THE ADDRESS.

Anthony Burns

THE PRISON.

Anthony Burns became a symbol of Northern resistance to the Fugitive Slave Law when he was arrested in Boston after his escape. Despite attempts to free him, he was returned to his owner. The attempts to save Burns were among many rescues—some successful, some not—by Northerners determined to resist the law.

The U.S. government spent more than $100,000 to return Anthony Burns to his owner—not a feat it could afford to repeat again. Nor was the South happy at Burns's return—the enormity of the resistance to the Fugitive Slave Law seemed one more proof that the North and the South were too different to remain as one country. In the meantime, Burns was forced to spend five months in a Virginia prison with his hands and feet in chains before Northerners were able to purchase his freedom. He became a minister, but, weak in health because of all he had endured, he died at the age of twenty-eight.

In 1854—the same year that Anthony Burns made and lost his bid for freedom—Congress passed the Kansas-Nebraska Act, another attempt to solve the question of slavery in the territories. Kansas and Nebraska were not yet states, but they were rapidly

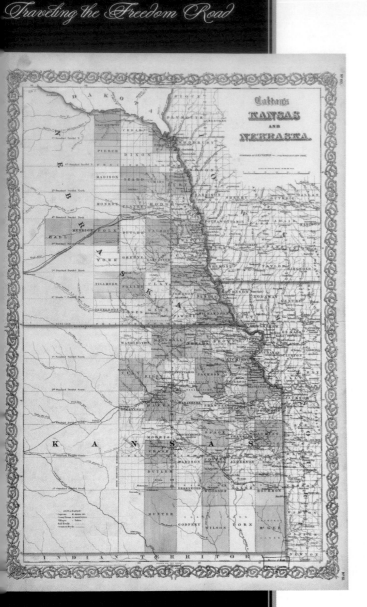

In 1854, Congress ruled that the people living in the Kansas and Nebraska territories could decide for themselves whether slavery should be legal. Thousands of settlers came to the territories, some supported by Northern abolitionists and some by Southern slaveholders, to build up a majority on their side.

filling up with both pro-slavery and anti-slavery settlers. Congress decided that the settlers themselves would choose whether Kansas and Nebraska would enter the Union as slave or free states. In Kansas, vicious fighting broke out between those for and those against slavery. The territory became known as "bleeding Kansas." Some abolitionists, who had for years protested peacefully, were now willing to use violence to end slavery.

The next huge crisis came in 1858, with the U.S. Supreme Court's decision in *Scott v. Sanford*. Dred Scott, a slave who had worked for his owner in several free states, argued that he had the right to be free according to the laws of those states (although not according to the 1850 Fugitive Slave Law). The Supreme Court said that Scott had no right even to sue for freedom, because as a slave he was not a citizen of the United States, but *property*. Here, again, was the heart of the matter—whether a slave was property or a human being.

For some abolitionists, when the Supreme Court took the side of property, it was the end of talk and reasoning. They felt that an armed attack was the only way to end slavery. In 1859, a white man named John Brown led five black men and sixteen white men in a raid on Harpers Ferry, Virginia (now in West Virginia), where he planned to steal government guns to start a rebellion. He was caught and hanged. Before he died, Brown told the Virginia court where he was tried: "This Court acknowledges too . . . the validity of the LAW OF GOD. I saw a book kissed, which I suppose to be the BIBLE . . . which teaches me that, 'All things whatsoever I would that men should do to me, I should do even so to them.' It teaches me further, to 'Remember them that are in bonds.' . . . I endeavored to act up to that instruction. . . . I believe that to have interfered as I have done . . . in behalf of [God's] *despised poor*, I have done no wrong, but RIGHT."

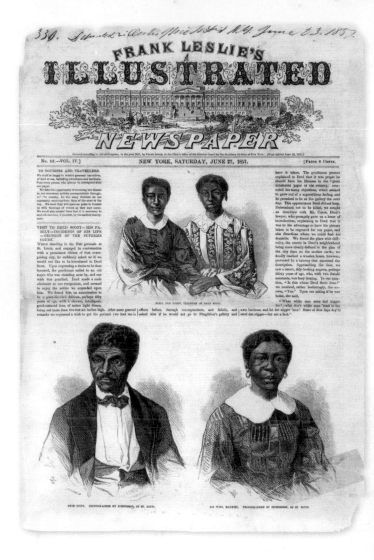

Dred Scott and his wife, Harriet, shown here with their daughters Eliza and Lizzie (above, center), sued for their freedom in 1846 because their owner had taken them to live in a free state and a free territory. Chief Justice Roger Taney of the Supreme Court declared in 1858 that they could not be free because African Americans were "altogether unfit to associate with the white race . . . and so far inferior that they had no rights which the white man was bound to respect."

To many in the North, John Brown was a hero; in the South he and his followers were deeply feared. There were far greater numbers of slaves than there were slave owners; the possibility of rebellion frightened many whites in the slave states. Yet this seemed to make them defend slavery even more as the only way to protect whites and control the situation.

The United States was not at peace with itself; slavery was tearing it in half. At the Myrtilla Miner School for Free Colored Girls in Washington, D.C., one student predicted the trouble to come. "I sometimes think that slavery will never be abolished, and then I nearly despair of freedom's swaying its banner over a suffering world," wrote Marietta Hill. "Sometimes a dark cloud seems to overshadow me . . . & I say, will slavery forever exist? But a voice says, 'It shall cease! It shall and must be abolished!' I think there will be blood shed before all can be free, and the question is, are we willing to give up our lives for it?"

The stormy 1850s came to an end with the election of Abraham Lincoln as president in 1860. Lincoln was a Northerner from the Republican Party. Many in the slave states thought he wanted to abolish slavery. This was not true; he simply did not want slavery to spread. Even so, his election became the last straw. The state of South Carolina seceded—it left the Union. Ten states followed: Mississippi, Florida, Alabama, Georgia, Louisiana, Texas, Virginia, Arkansas, North Carolina, and Tennessee. Their actions meant the United States was no longer a single country. These states believed that each state could make its own laws. They refused to be ruled by the U.S. government anymore. Four slave states did not secede: Maryland, Delaware, Kentucky, and Missouri.

Abraham Lincoln could have let the seceded states go, but he believed in the Union. He believed that Americans shared more than they disagreed on. He thought one union made the country strong. So when South Carolina attacked a U.S. Army fort in Charleston Harbor on April 14, 1861, Lincoln went to war. He said that he was not fighting to end slavery; he was fighting to save the Union. Abolitionists and those who were pro-slavery; blacks and whites; the enslaved and the free in every state—indeed, around the world—waited to see what would happen.

ABRAHAM LINCOLN AND HIS SON THAD.

Dear Teacher,

I sometimes think that slavery will never be abolished, & then I nearly despair of freedom's swaying its banner over a suffering world. Sometimes a dark cloud seems to overshadow me; and since the Nebraska bill has passed the cloud appears thicker & darker — & I say, will slavery forever exist? But a voice says "It shall cease" "It shall and must be abolished"! I think there will be blood shed before all can be free, and the question is are we willing to give up our lives for

freedom? Will we die for our people? We may say yes. But I fear our hearts would grow sick at the thought, if we knew it must be. Life we know is dear, and there are many things to bind us to life. Yet the Saviour gave his life for us; tho' he, even he said, "O my Father, if it be possible, let this cup pass from me! Nevertheless, not as I will, but as thou wilt"! The Saviour truly said of his disciples "The spirit indeed is willing, but the flesh is weak"! & I fear we too may be found sleeping in the fearful hour of freedom's betrayal!
In great faith, yet blended with fear.
Most truly,
Marietta T. Hill.

Washington D.C. July 5, 1854.

ABOVE *Abraham Lincoln, shown here with his son Thad, disliked slavery and did not want it to spread beyond the Southern states. After he was elected president in 1860, states in the South seceded from the United States, fearing that Lincoln would abolish slavery.*

LEFT *As a classroom assignment, Marietta Hill wrote this letter in 1854, predicting that there would be a war before slavery could be abolished. She was a student at the Myrtilla Miner School for Free Colored Girls in Washington, D.C.*

Soon after the Civil War began, this enslaved family on Smith's Plantation in Beaufort, South Carolina, posed for photographer Timothy O'Sullivan. O'Sullivan was one of several photographers who covered the war. Their photographs gave Northerners a vivid picture of people and events.

THE CIVIL WAR

JUST BEFORE THE WAR, A WHITE PREACHER CAME TO us slaves and said: 'Do you want to keep your homes where you get all to eat, and raise your children, or do you want to be free to roam round without a home, like the wild animals? If you want to keep your homes you better pray for the South to win. All that want to pray for the South to win, raise [your] hand.' We all raised our hands 'cause we were scared not to, but we sure didn't want the South to win," remembered William Adams, who was a young slave in Texas when the Civil War started. White people might have thought they were fighting for the right of a state to remain in or leave the Union, but African Americans understood that the war was about freedom.

The eleven states that had seceded formed a new country, the Confederate States of America. Its constitution was very much like the U.S. Constitution, except that it clearly allowed slavery. Jefferson Davis, the president of the Confederacy, often said that the war was not about slavery, but about the right of a state to make its own rules.

This 1862 map of the United States shows the Union free states and territories in blue-green, the seceded states and territory in pink, and the border states and slaveholding territories that did not secede in yellow.

But Alexander Stephens, the vice president of the Confederacy, declared that the new Confederate government's "foundations are laid, its cornerstone rests upon the great truth, that the negro [black man] is not equal to the white man; that slavery—subordination to the superior race—is his natural and normal condition."

Free blacks in the North were ready to prove Stephens wrong. They were eager to serve in the U.S. (Union) army, but for two years, until 1863, the government refused their services. Racial prejudice still existed in the North. Some people believed that black men could not follow orders or fight well; others, that they shouldn't be given guns. President Lincoln feared that if African Americans became soldiers, the

Mansion of the Rebel Gen¹ Thomas F. Drayton
Hilton Head
S.C.

Most of the fighting of the Civil War took place in the South, where enslaved people lived in the midst of army camps, marching soldiers, and battles. This photograph of the home of Confederate general Thomas Drayton in Hilton Head, South Carolina, shows an African American woman and several Union soldiers after the Union succeeded in capturing the area.

four Southern states that had not seceded—called the border states—would leave the Union after all. Black Americans were frustrated and angered by his decision, but they still supported the war. They formed their own unofficial military units and practiced drilling, to be ready for the time when their services would be accepted.

Northern blacks might have been prevented from fighting, but most blacks in the South could not avoid the war. Except for the Battle of Gettysburg, fought in Pennsylvania in July 1863, the major battles of the war took place in the South. It seemed that both Union and Confederate soldiers were camped or marching or looking for food and supplies nearly everywhere. "Next thing we knew there were Confederate soldiers riding by pretty nearly every day in big droves," said Isaac Adams, a young slave in Louisiana when the Civil War started. "Sometimes they would come and buy corn and wheat and hogs, but they never did take any . . . like the Yankees [Union soldiers] did later on."

RIGHT *Like many people in the South, slaves risked being in the line of fire from Union soldiers. Here, early in the war (1862), Union soldiers of the Fourth New York Heavy Artillery load a cannon in Arlington, Virginia.*

OPPOSITE *In the confusion of war, African American families like the one in this photograph escaped to Union army camps. Here they are crossing the Rappahannock River in Virginia. Timothy O'Sullivan took this photo in August 1862.*

Under Fire

Cato Carter of Alabama remembered living right on the edge of war. "I have seen the trees bend low and shake all over and heard the roar and the popping of cannon balls," he said. "There was killing going on so terrible like people were dogs."

Another enslaved child, Rachel Cruze, who spent the war in east Tennessee, recalled, "One day a man—a most foolish one—rode into our yard on a white horse and proceeded toward the barn. I ran after him to see what he was going to do and, just as I got there, a cannon ball fell a few feet from me, covering the horse and rider and myself with black dirt. The [lookouts] at the fort across the river had recognized him as a Johnny [Confederate soldier], but seeing me follow him had thrown the ball wide just

to give him warning and to save hitting me. That Johnny, when he got his breath, went lickety split down the road. . . . The officer in charge at the fort then sent old Major [her owner] a note asking him to keep 'that child' out of sight so I wouldn't get hurt."

"Those cannons were terrible things," Rachel Cruze also commented, "holding about a half bushel of powder, and then the gunners would put heavy iron log chains in, and iron pots. They waited until all the enemy down below was in the water and then they let them have the full effect of that awful blast. The river turned red with the slaughter."

In the turmoil of war, some slaves stayed on their plantations, some were brought to Confederate army camps to work for Southern soldiers, and some were moved farther west so that Yankee soldiers could not take them and their white owners would be safe from the worst fighting. Many slaves took the chance to run away to the Union army camps, where they hoped to gain freedom. Mary Barbour was an enslaved child when her father woke her up in the middle of the night,

dressing me in the dark, all the time telling me to keep quiet.... After we were dressed he went outside and peeped round for a minute.... We snuck out of the house and along the woods path.... I reckon I will always remember that walk, with the bushes slapping my legs, the wind sighing in the trees, and the hoot owls and whippoorwills hollering.... I was half asleep and scared stiff, but in a little while we passed the ... thicket and there were the mules and wagon. There was a quilt in the bottom of the wagon, and on this they laid we youngins.... As we rode along I listened to pappy and mammy talk.... Pappy says that we are going to join the Yankees. We traveled all night and hid in the woods all day for a long time.... When we got to New Bern the Yankees took the mules and wagon ... and put us on a long white boat named *Ocean Waves* and to Roanoke [Virginia] we go.... My pappy was a shoemaker, so he makes Yankee boots, and we get along pretty good.

383.   **A Group of "Contrabands."**
[FOR DESCRIPTION OF THIS VIEW SEE THE OTHER SIDE OF THIS CARD.]

Former slaves at Foller's Farm in Cumberland, Virginia, sit in front of a cabin, photographed by James Gibson on May 14, 1862. They were now contrabands, fugitive slaves who were no longer forced to work for their owners but who often aided the Union army.

In the early months of the war, Northern soldiers returned some of these runaway slaves to their owners. But Union general Benjamin Butler decided that it was fair to keep them, just as it was customary, in war, to take—or "commandeer"—food, animals, shelter, and other property from civilians when soldiers needed them. Butler called the fugitive slaves who made it to Union camps "contraband of war." Congress passed laws in 1861 and 1862 legally recognizing Butler's decision. Contrabands did not go back to their plantations, but usually helped to cook, clean, build fortifications, and generally aid the Union army.

John Finnely was twelve years old when he ran away from his owner in Northern Alabama. Ten of the slaves on his plantation had already fled, and none had been captured. He left with only a hunk of meat and some cornbread and was "half scared to death." He kept off the roads and moved as quietly as he could through the woods. Just once, he hid in a thicket from white patrollers who were only steps away. He held his breath, and they didn't see him. When John finally made it to the Union camp, he found that all ten of the other enslaved men were also there: They were all now contrabands. They were sent by train to Stevenson, Alabama, where they built breastworks—walls of logs, soil, rocks, and whatever else the men could find in the area to pile high enough to protect the Union soldiers.

At the Union army's Camp Brightwood in Washington, D.C., three contrabands pose with officers of the Second Rhode Island Volunteer Infantry.

John Finnely stayed in Stevenson only a few days before he was sent to Nashville, Tennessee. There he carried water for the men posted at the Union army headquarters, until a battle started. "The noise was awful, just one steady roar of the guns and the cannons," he recounted many years later. "The window glass in Nashville was all shook out from the . . . cannons. There were dead men all over the ground and lots of wounded and some cussin' and some prayin'. Some were moanin' and this and that one cried for . . . water and, God Allmighty, I don't want [to see] any such again."

Men, women, and children were all on the move—braving the danger of being captured, of being caught up in battle—to become contrabands, to be one step closer to freedom. The Union army often set up camps for contrabands near their own camps. Schools sprang up for these ex-slaves that both children and grown-

Contrabands wait to begin work for the Union army's Quartermaster Corps, which was responsible for getting supplies to the soldiers and building and maintaining camps. These contrabands were photographed on a wharf in Alexandria, Virginia, by photographer Mathew Brady.

ups attended. Mary Chase, a free black woman, started the first one in Alexandria, Virginia. Some former slaves, like Lorenzo Ezell, learned on their own. "I've never been to school but I just picked up reading," he said. "With some [of the] first money I ever earned, I bought . . . an old blue-black Webster. I carried that book wherever I [went]. When I plowed down a row, I stopped at the end to rest and then I [looked over] the lesson."

Contrabands did many jobs for the Union army. They acted as scouts, guides, and spies for Union forces. Harriet Tubman, the well-known "conductor" for the Underground Railroad, worked as a Northern spy for three years in South Carolina. Some did laundry, served as drivers, and cooked for the soldiers. Men and older boys were needed "to help clear roads and build temp'rary bridges," explained Thomas Cole, who ran away from Alabama to Tennessee. "We walked miles on muddy ground, crossed rivers, wading [into] water up to our chins. We built rafts and pole bridges to get the mules and horses and cannons across, and up and down hills, and cut roads through timber." Women, children, and elderly men who could not do heavy labor were moved back to plantations whose owners had fled the war. Northern white men or Southern men who had agreed to be loyal to the Union ran these plantations. Workers received wages, but they were often low.

A Step Toward Freedom

By the fall of 1862, more than a year after the war started, there was no end to it in sight. The Union had lost several important battles, including two at Bull Run (Manassas), Virginia, and three in Virginia's Shenandoah Valley (McDowell, Cross Keys, Port Republic). They had won, or held off, the Confederacy at Shiloh, Tennessee, and Antietam (Sharpsburg), Maryland, but had done so at the cost of thousands of lives. Still, the victory at Antietam gave President Lincoln the boost he needed to announce that on January 1, 1863, he would issue a proclamation to emancipate—to free forever—the slaves in the Confederacy.

Excitement grew in free black communities and among abolitionists as January 1 approached. Many slaves lived too far away from Washington, D.C., to have heard the news, and slave owners were not likely to tell them. But some did, and word spread from person to person as each acknowledged its importance. The Emancipation Proclamation marked the first time that the United States government took a stand to support the principles of freedom and equality in the U.S. Constitution and the Declaration of Independence for all men. It stated, "Now, therefore I, Abraham Lincoln . . . do order and declare that all persons held as slaves within

Ent'd according to Act of Congress, A. D. 1863, by W. T. Carlton, in the Clerk's Office of the District Court of the District of Mass.

This card pictures a group of African Americans gathering around a man holding a watch on December 31, 1862. They wait in excitement for midnight, January 1, 1863, when the Emancipation Proclamation will be issued.

said designated States [the Confederacy] . . . are, and henceforward shall be free; and that the Executive government of the United States, including the military and naval authorities thereof, will recognize and maintain the freedom of said persons." After the Emancipation Proclamation was issued, contrabands, appropriately, were called freedmen.

Henry M. Turner, the African American pastor of the Israel Bethel Church in Washington, D.C., would never forget January 1, 1863. "Seeing such a multitude of people in and around my church, I hurriedly went up to the office of the first paper in which the proclamation of freedom could be printed, known as the 'Evening Star,' and squeezed myself through the dense crowd that was waiting for the paper," he wrote.

Thomas Nast, a famous artist of the time, created this print to celebrate emancipation. On the left are scenes from slavery, including a slave auction. On the right are scenes of freedom, where children go to school and a man is paid for his work. At the center is a happy African American family, and below them Abraham Lincoln, who issued the Emancipation Proclamation.

The first sheet run off with the proclamation in it was grabbed for by three of us, but some active young man got possession of it and fled. The next sheet was grabbed for by several, and was torn into tatters. The third sheet from the press was grabbed for by several, but I succeeded in procuring so much of it as contained the proclamation, and off I went for life and death.

Down Pennsylvania Avenue I ran as for my life, and when the people saw me coming with the paper in my hand they raised a shouting cheer that was almost deafening. As many as could get around me lifted me to a great platform, and I started to read the proclamation. I had run the best of a mile, I was out of breath, and could not read. Mr. Hinton, to whom I handed the paper, read it with great force and clearness. While he was reading every kind of demonstration and gesticulation was going on. Men squealed, women fainted, dogs barked, white and colored people shook hands, songs were sung, and by this time cannons began to fire at the navy-yard, and follow in the wake of the roar that had for some time been going on behind the White House.... Great processions of colored and white men marched to and fro and passed in front of the White House and congratulated President Lincoln on his proclamation. The President came to the window and made responsive bows, and thousands told him, if he would come out of that palace, they would hug him to death.... It was indeed a time of times, and a half time, nothing like it will ever be seen again in this life.

African Americans were pleased with the Emancipation Proclamation, but some were cautious about what it would actually do. Lincoln was not freeing slaves in the border states, just in the Confederacy. He still feared that the border states would join the Confederacy if he did so. Further, Lincoln was not stating that slavery itself was wrong. He felt there were limits on what he could accomplish. As he wrote in response to a petition from a group of children that he free *all* children who were enslaved: "Please tell these little people I am very glad their young hearts are so full of just and generous sympathy. While I have not the power to grant all they ask, I trust they will remember that God has, and that, as it seems, He wills to do it." Nevertheless, the Emancipation Proclamation became a beacon of hope.

The Emancipation Proclamation allowed black soldiers to serve in the Union army.

The proclamation also contained one more announcement that would change the course of slavery and the lives of African Americans. Black men were now allowed to join the Union army. (The navy had accepted black sailors from the beginning of the war.) For Lincoln, this was a sensible decision, since it added a new, large group of soldiers to fight for the United States. The Confederacy had no large pool to draw on, because it would never give hundreds of thousands of slaves weapons to fight. (Although toward the end of the war, in 1865, the Confederate Congress did agree to recruit black soldiers, but it was too late to use them effectively.) The chance to fight for the freedom of their brothers and sisters gave black Americans a sense of pride and determination. They were ready to prove

themselves in battle. Many black men who enlisted were free, but a good portion of them had earlier been slaves.

On May 22, 1863, the U.S. War Department established the Bureau of Colored Troops to recruit black soldiers from each state and organize them into units. These units would be all black, but they would be led by white officers. Traditional prejudices were still in place—white and black soldiers were trained in and fought in separate regiments, and African Americans were not chosen as commanders. In fact, there was still a great deal of prejudice in the North about recruiting

ABOVE RIGHT *This sailor, Charles Batties, is one of many African Americans who served in the Union navy. Unlike the army, the navy had accepted African American enlistments before the Emancipation Proclamation, from the beginning of the Civil War.*

ABOVE LEFT *Young African Americans also did their part to help the Union win the Civil War. Here an orderly sits on a horse belonging to Union general John A. Rawlings. The photograph was taken on June 14, 1864.*

black soldiers at all, including among white soldiers. "We can remember, when we first enlisted, it was hardly safe for us to pass by the camps to Beaufort [South Carolina] and back," recalled Thomas Long about the white troops who harassed him and other black soldiers of the First South Carolina Volunteers.

But blacks enlisted despite these limitations—186,000 African Americans fought in the Civil War. "We lived it down by our natural manhood," said Long about white prejudice, "and now the white soldiers take us by the hand and say Brother Soldier.... If we hadn't become soldiers ... our freedom might have slipped through the two houses of Congress and President Lincoln's four years might have passed by and nothing been done for us. But now things can never go back, because we have showed our energy and our courage and our natural manhood."

Some black soldiers first came to the Union army as contrabands. Richard Slaughter was about fourteen years old when his enslaved family arrived in Hampton, Virginia, in 1862. "The Yankees burned Hampton and the [U.S. naval] fleet went up the James River. My father and mother and cousins went aboard the *Meritania* with me," he explained. "The gun boats would fire on the towns and plantations and run the white folks off. After that they would carry all the colored folks back down here to Old Point and put them behind Union lines." Slaughter worked carrying water, traveling up and down the rivers. At one point, "I left the creek aboard a steamer, the *General Hooker*, and went to Alexandria, Va. Abraham Lincoln came aboard the steamer and we carried him to Mt. Vernon, George Washington's old home. What did he look like? Why, he looked more like an old preacher than anything I know."

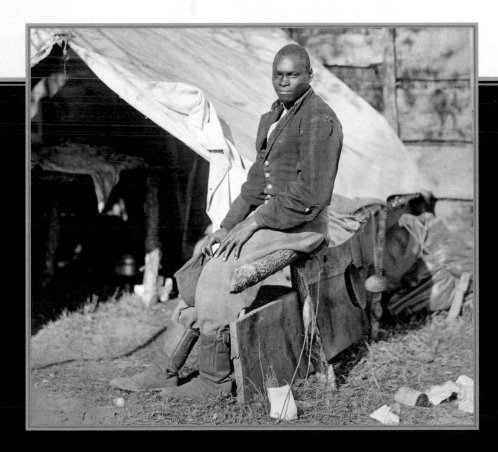

LEFT *John Henry, a servant to the U.S. Army, sits outside a tent at the headquarters of the Third Army Corps in October 1863.*

OPPOSITE *Company E of the Fourth U.S. Colored Infantry stand with their rifles at Fort Lincoln, near Washington, D.C. Mathew Brady took this photograph circa 1863.*

Slaughter enlisted in the Union army at Baltimore, Maryland, in 1864. He was "about seventeen years old then. . . . I was assigned to the Nineteenth Regiment of Maryland Company B. While I was training, they fought at Petersburg [Virginia]. . . . They took Richmond. . . . [On] that day I walked up the road in Richmond [with the victorious troops]. . . . I have never been wounded," he reflected years later. "My clothes have been cut off me by bullets but the Lord kept them off my back, I guess."

Tens of thousands of black soldiers, however, died in the Civil War. They had even more to risk than white soldiers, since the Confederate government said it would not take them as prisoners of war, but would shoot or enslave them. African American soldiers were assigned more heavy-labor tasks (like hauling and construction) than white soldiers, while still participating in combat. Although they were promised pay equal to what white soldiers earned, for months they were paid considerably less. Some even refused any pay, rather than accept less, although they continued to serve.

"Why are we not worth as much as white soldiers?" wrote one black private to his sister.

We do the same work they do, and do what they cannot. We fight as well as they do. . . . Why is it that they do not want to give us our pay when they have already witnessed our deeds of courage and bravery? . . . They want to come around and say we are laborers. If we are laborers, how is it then we do soldiers' duty, such as stand guard, and do picket duty and form a line of battle. . . . No, because we are men of color, they are trying to impose upon us.

African American sharpshooters for the Union army drill near Dutch Gap, Virginia, in November 1864.

It wasn't until June 15, 1864, that Congress passed a law guaranteeing blacks and whites the same pay for military service.

Blacks in Battle

But despite discrimination and prejudice inside and outside the military, black soldiers built up an outstanding record as disciplined and fierce fighters. On May 27, 1863, African American soldiers stormed Confederate fortifications at Port Hudson, Louisiana. After this battle, the *New York Times* wrote, "It is no longer possible to doubt the bravery and steadiness of the colored race." (Even in praise, the white press did not fail to point out that black soldiers were not simply men, but of a different race.) On June 7 at Milliken's Bend, Louisiana, four newly formed regiments of freedmen without good weapons kept Confederate soldiers from destroying a crucial supply line. Thirty-five percent of the black soldiers that fought there were killed.

African American soldiers of the Fifty-Fourth Massachusetts Colored Infantry lead the assault on Fort Wagner, a Confederate stronghold near Charleston, South Carolina. Many were killed, including their white commander, Colonel Robert Gould Shaw, whom Confederates buried with his men.

On July 18, 1863, the Fifty-Fourth Massachusetts Colored Infantry, perhaps the best known African American regiment of the Civil War, attacked Fort Wagner, near Charleston, South Carolina. Under heavy fire, some of the soldiers managed to climb part of the wall before they were all beaten back. Forty percent of the men were killed. Two days after the battle, Frederick Douglass's son Lewis, who was a sergeant in the Fifty-Fourth, wrote, "Not a man flinched, though it was a trying time. Men fell all around me. A shell would explode and clear a space of twenty feet, our men would close up again, but it was no use[;] we had to retreat, which was a very hazardous undertaking. How I got out of that fight alive I cannot tell, but I am here. Remember if I die I die in a good cause. I wish we had a hundred thousand colored troops[;] we would put an end to this war."

At Fort Pillow, Tennessee, in April 1864, black soldiers—and some whites who fought near them—who had surrendered were killed by Confederates, rather than taken as prisoners of war. "Remember Fort Pillow" became a battle cry, especially for African Americans. Black soldiers were also killed in great numbers at the Battle of the Crater, near Petersburg, Virginia, on July 30, 1864. But on February 18, 1865, African American soldiers were the first to march into Charleston, South Carolina, when the city was taken by Union forces. "Words would fail to describe the scene . . . the welcome given to a regiment of colored troops by their people redeemed from slavery," remembered Charles Fox, the colonel of a black regiment. "As shouts, prayers, and blessings resounded . . . all felt that the hardships and dangers . . . were fully re-paid. . . . Cheers, blessings, prayers, and songs were heard on every side." Black troops were also the first to march into Richmond, Virginia, the Confederate capital, on April 2, after Confederate soldiers left the city in retreat.

The Civil War ended days later, on April 9, 1865, when the South's forces surrendered at Appomattox Court House in Virginia. But on April 14, President Lincoln was shot while he was watching a play at Ford's Theatre in Washington, D.C., and died the next morning. Andrew Johnson, the vice president from Tennessee, a Southerner who had been loyal to the Union, became the new president. And before the end of that year, *all* enslaved people were truly emancipated. On December 18, 1865, the Thirteenth Amendment, abolishing slavery everywhere in the United States, became part of the U.S. Constitution.

Huge areas of the South were destroyed during the Civil War, including the cities of Atlanta, Georgia; Richmond, Virginia; and Charleston, South Carolina. Here, four children sit in view of ruined buildings seen through the porch of a church at 150 Meeting Street in Charleston. The photograph was taken in April 1865, the month the war ended.

RECONSTRUCTION

AFTER FOUR YEARS OF CIVIL WAR, THE CONFEDERACY had been worn down—it had not had enough supplies or soldiers to continue fighting. Much of its land was damaged because armies had camped there or battles had been fought there. Life was hard for both black and white Americans living in the South. "Talk about hard times!" said Andrew Moss, who had been a slave and was thirteen years old at the end of the war. "We saw them in those days, during the War and most especially after the surrender. . . . We were glad to eat ash cakes and drink parched corn and rye instead of coffee. I saw my grandmother go to the smokehouse and scrape up the dirt where the meat had dropped off and took it to the house for seasoning."

In 1865, then, there was no doubt that the South needed reconstructing. "Reconstruction" means to rebuild something that has been destroyed. Not only the land and cities of the South needed to be restored—so did the union of states. Eleven states had deliberately left the Union, which Lincoln and the Northern states

This sketch shows African Americans gathering firewood in the hard days after the Civil War, to keep warm during winter in Virginia. Once slaves, after 1865 they were free, but many struggled to find food and shelter.

considered illegal. How were they to be made part of the United States again? Should people who had fought in the Confederate army or led the Confederate government be able to vote or serve in Congress? Should the U.S. government aid white Southerners who were suffering from hunger and poverty?

After Abraham Lincoln was assassinated and Andrew Johnson was sworn in as president, Johnson, not Lincoln, was the man who made decisions about the future of the North and South. Lincoln had been far more popular than Johnson. War was a great sorrow to Lincoln, and when peace finally came, he wanted to heal the wounds of the broken country and to take care of all people in need. Johnson, who had owned slaves himself, was not as concerned with the rights of those who had once been enslaved. He did not get along with many of the Northern congressmen who wanted to help the freedmen and who wished to deny the right to vote and hold political office to those who had led the Confederacy.

Most important, Johnson was deeply prejudiced against African Americans, and he did not believe they should be granted civil rights or have a role in politics. He wanted to quickly restore to the ex-Confederate states their full rights as states in the Union, including the right to elect members to Congress who could pass new laws for the entire country. Johnson hoped that Southerners who had been loyal to the Union, not wealthy Confederate leaders, would run these state governments, but he accepted the fact that ex-Confederates came to dominate them.

As one of the consequences of leaving the Union, many Confederates were not allowed to vote right after the Civil War. However, Johnson pardoned thousands of people who had served the Confederate government, allowing them the right to vote again. He asked the Southern states to write new state constitutions—they did, and he was not troubled when none of these documents

Andrew Johnson became president of the United States after Abraham Lincoln was assassinated. Once a slave owner, Johnson had little sympathy for the freedmen. His plan for Reconstruction made it easy for the seceded states to re-enter the Union.

gave any rights to the freedmen. When elections for Southern state governors and state lawmakers were held in the fall of 1866, almost everyone elected had served in the Confederate government.

Johnson was opposed by a group of white congressmen, nicknamed the Radical Republicans because they believed in full and immediate political rights for the freedmen and penalties for the ex-Confederate states. Representative Thaddeus Stevens of Pennsylvania and Massachusetts senator Charles Sumner were among the best-known Radical Republican leaders. Under them, the U.S. Congress rejected the first round of Southern state constitutions and refused to let the first congressmen elected in the South be part of Congress. They would not accept states back into the Union until they had written constitutions that clearly ended slavery and gave the freedmen political rights.

Therefore, in 1867, Congress, which was controlled by Radical Republicans and which represented the Northern states, divided the former Confederate states into five districts, each run by a U.S. military commander. U.S. soldiers occupied the South—to

This two-story building provided housing for freedmen in New Bern, North Carolina.

keep the peace, enforce the law, and protect the freedmen. The military commanders made sure that freedmen could register to vote. Not only did the freedmen need protection, but black soldiers themselves were targets of white violence. Right after the Civil War, Union soldiers had remained in the South to keep order, and a considerable number were African American.

In 1866, riots against blacks in Memphis, Tennessee, and New Orleans, Louisiana, killed or wounded several hundred people. Yet the Southern states were bitterly opposed to having the U.S. Army govern them. They called this "bayonet rule," meaning weapons—military force—were being used to control them. They wanted the right to govern themselves, which included treating black people in any way they chose, denying them their rights.

Just keeping a force of U.S. soldiers in the Southern states was not unusual, however. U.S. soldiers were on duty in every state, even during peacetime. In the nineteenth century, federal soldiers fought against American Indians and guarded the Atlantic and Pacific coastlines with support from the South. What the Southern states objected to was the use of federal troops to police *them* for discriminating against freedmen. Yet Congress was not harsh in this respect. Before the Radical Republicans passed laws for Reconstruction, the number of U.S. soldiers in the South had already dropped dramatically from about 200,000 troops to only about 20,000. By 1867, the majority of black soldiers had been discharged from the army and no longer policed the South at all.

By 1870, all the Southern states had been readmitted to the Union. In that year, only about 9,000 U.S. soldiers remained in the South. They were spread widely over the countryside. For example, Arkansas had only 164 soldiers, and North Carolina had 277 soldiers in the whole state. From 1870 to 1877, U.S. soldiers would be called in only occasionally to quell extreme violence against the freedmen and the whites who supported them. In 1876, 6,011 U.S. troops remained on duty in the South, and over half of these were stationed in Texas.

Under Radical Reconstruction, however, Congress did expect the Southern states to give African American men a vote in electing delegates to write new state constitutions. These new constitutions also had to guarantee African American men the right to vote in state elections. (Neither white nor black women were allowed to vote at this time.) Only then could the Southern states regain their rights as states within the Union. The South was not happy about this, but each formerly seceded state did follow these rules. By the end of July 1870, every ex-Confederate state had been readmitted to the Union and could now send senators and representatives to

Artist Alfred R. Waud drew this sketch of a freedmen's village in Greene Heights, Arlington, Virginia, near Washington, D.C., which contained a schoolhouse, chapel, and old-age home. The U.S. Army established camps such as this to house African American refugees from the war, but most of these camps were closed soon after the war ended.

Congress to help make federal laws. On paper, these states also guaranteed rights to African Americans. But what would in fact happen to those who had been recently freed?

Fair at Last?

Black Americans believed that a fair Reconstruction would reunite their families, give them land to farm, allow them to work for themselves, grant them political rights, and give young and old an education. To help them reach these goals, on March 3, 1865, just before the Civil War ended, Congress established the Bureau of Refugees, Freedmen, and Abandoned Lands, called by everyone the Freedmen's Bureau. The

bureau distributed food and clothing, and it established schools and hospitals. The bureau also assisted Southern whites who were poor and homeless after the war. Congress also started a savings bank for African Americans, the Freedmen's Savings and Trust Company. In the new, truly *United* States, it was hoped that those who had once been enslaved would be able to earn and save money to build for the future.

For a time after it was established, some freedmen did not know about the Freedmen's Bureau. Some didn't even know they were free. News traveled slowly, and slaveholders did not always tell their slaves. Because there was little information, slaves were sometimes unclear about what to do next. They owned no land, no businesses, no houses. Yet this is what Tom Robinson, a teenager enslaved in Texas, felt when he heard about emancipation:

One day I was out milking the cows. Mr. Dave [his owner] came down into the field and he had a paper in his hands. "Listen to me, Tom," he said. "Listen to what I read you." And he read from a paper all about how I was free. You can't tell how I felt. "You're joking me," I said. "No, I ain't," says he, "you're free." "No," says I, "it's a joke." "No," says he, "it's a law that I got to read this paper to you. Now listen while I read it again."

But still I wouldn't believe him. "Just go up to the house," says he, "and ask Mrs. Robinson [Dave's wife]. She'll tell you." So I went. "It's a joke," I says to her. "Did you ever know your master to tell you a lie?"

she says. "No," says I, "I ain't." "Well," she says, "the War's over and you're free."

By that time I thought maybe she was telling me what was right. "[Mrs.] Robinson," says I, "can I go over to see the Smiths?"—they were a colored family that lived nearby. "Don't you understand," says she, "you're free. You don't have to ask me what you can do. Run along, child." And so I went. And do you know why I was a going? I wanted to find out if they were free too. I just couldn't take it all in. I couldn't believe we were all free alike.

Was I happy? Lord! You can take anything. No matter how good you treat it—it wants to be free. You can treat it good and feed it and give it everything it seems to want—but if you open the cage—it's happy.

Once slaves living near Washington, D.C., this family was free at the end of the Civil War. Most freedmen wanted to work together as families on their own farms without following the orders of white owners.

A HAPPY FAMILY.

ABOVE Harper's Weekly *ran this print of an African American mother with seven children, all looking cheerful, in 1866. Northern white readers seeing it would think that freedmen's families were happy. Although this family was depicted together, many families were separated under slavery and never saw each other again.*

OPPOSITE *Freed at the war's end, these African Americans worked on Aiken's farm on the James River in Virginia. Some freedmen left the plantations they had labored on as slaves, but others continued to work for their former owners so that they would have a secure place to live.*

"I reckon I was glad to get free, because I knew then that I [wouldn't] wake up some morning to find that my mammy or some of the rest of my family [had been] sold," said Charlie Barbour of North Carolina. One of the things African Americans wanted most during Reconstruction was to reunite families that had been brutally broken apart under slavery. Husbands and wives were looking everywhere for each other, and mothers and fathers were searching for their children. The Freedmen's Bureau helped former slaves locate family members. "They had a passion, not for wandering, as for getting together, and every mother's son among them seemed to be in search of his mother; every mother in search of her children," noted one South Carolina Freedmen's Bureau agent. "In their eyes the work of emancipation was incomplete until the families which had been dispersed by slavery were reunited."

Ben Dodson was fortunate; after twenty years of separation, he found his wife, Betty, in a camp for refugees after the war. "Glory! Glory! Hallelujah! This is my Betty, sure. I found you at last," he exclaimed. "I hunted and hunted until I tracked you up here. I was bound to hunt till I found you if you were alive." But the chances of reunion were small without knowledge of where loved ones had been sold or what they looked like after years of being apart. Black newspapers, which grew in number after the Civil War, carried ads like this one: "Information Wanted, of Caroline Dodson, who was sold from Nashville, Nov. 1st, 1862, by James Lumsden to Warwick, (a trader then in human beings), who carried her to Atlanta, Georgia. . . . Any information of her whereabouts will be thankfully received and rewarded by her mother. Lucinda Lowery, Nashville." Many African Americans, however, never saw members of their families again.

Freedmen and -women who were together rushed to make their marriages legal. Instead of slave owners setting the rules, African American men were now legally the heads of their families. Women, who had once been forced to work in the fields, could

While some freedmen were initially given land by the U.S. government, much of this land was given back to Confederate families by 1870. These freedmen pick cotton in Louisiana or Mississippi sometime after 1880, in a photograph by William Henry Jackson. It is not known if they worked their own land, or if they worked for others for wages or a share of the crop.

spend more time caring for their children, although their labor was still needed to farm. To bring in money, some women worked as domestics in the homes of whites. One contract called for the African American employee "to do cooking, washing, ironing, and general housework and anything about the yard or garden that may be required of her." Black women frequently looked after white children.

But more than anything else, the newly freed slaves wanted their own land. Many believed that land was owed to them after the years of work to make it fruitful. "The property they [white Southerners] hold was nearly all earned by the sweat of our brows," said a freedman from Alabama. A Virginia freedman argued, "We have a right to the land where we are located. . . . Our wives, our children, our husbands, have been sold over and over again to purchase the lands we now locate upon; for that reason we have a divine right to the land."

Some U.S. Army officers, congressmen, and agents of the Freedmen's Bureau wanted to settle blacks on their own land. Union general William Tecumseh Sherman, worrying about how to feed the large number of slaves escaping behind Union lines, had issued an order in January 1865 giving each family forty acres of land. Although not specifically in the order, he also wanted the army to lend the former slaves mules to work their farms. Many freedmen believed that everyone would receive "forty acres and a mule" from the U.S. government. In fact, this did not happen.

Just after the war, some freedmen did receive land that had once been owned by Southern planters, who could not run their large plantations during the war. Sometimes the planters had simply abandoned their plantations as war came their way. In other cases, this land was confiscated—taken away—by the U.S. government because the owners could not pay their taxes. Most of this land was eventually returned to the original white owners. But African Americans made some progress. By 1900, 25 percent owned their land. Still, this left 75 percent of Southern blacks to make what living they could by working for someone else.

During Reconstruction, the vast majority of African Americans worked for wages or as sharecroppers. Sharecroppers grew their crops on part of someone else's land. They were allowed to keep a percentage of the crop they produced; the rest went to pay the landowner for use of the land. Isom Moseley from Georgia, nine years old at the end of the Civil War, grew up with stories about those times. "Well, now, they tell me it was a . . . year before the folks knew that . . . they were free," said Moseley years later. "And when they found out they were free, they worked on shares. . . .Worked on shares, didn't rent no land. . . . They got [a] third, I think they said, [of] what they made, after surrender."

Isom's friends and family got to keep a one-third share of the crop they raised, but some sharecroppers earned as little as a quarter of a share, and some earned even less. With the money they made from selling the crop, they would buy their supplies from the landowner. Sharecroppers had little or sometimes no money left over. Even worse, the freedmen often went into debt year after year, never able to pay off their balances and start fresh someplace else. Tied by debt to the farms they worked, the freedmen had little more ability to raise themselves up economically than they had had under slavery. This is what many white landowners intended. Even though African Americans were no longer slaves, they were bound to landowning whites because they had no other way to make a living.

Some freedmen did not sharecrop, but chose to work for wages, often for their former owners. Contracts with white employers were full of rules about how black workers should behave. They were to be quiet, hardworking, and orderly, as decided by the employer. Some contracts even said that workers could not have their friends stay overnight without permission.

These African Americans picking cotton may have worked for wages or shares. Often, the contracts they signed favored the owners of the land, as did laws passed by the Southern states. Most white people in the South accepted that the slaves had been freed, but wanted as much as possible to re-create the control they had of workers under slavery.

However, freedmen who worked for wages could ask a Freedmen's Bureau agent to help them draw up fair contracts and arrangements.

Robert Glenn was fifteen years old when

Master told me to catch two horses.... [W]e had to go to Dickenson, which was the county seat of Webster County [in Kentucky]. On the way ... he said to me, "Bob, did you know you are free and Lincoln has freed you? You are as free as I am." We went to the Freedmen's Bureau ... office. A Yankee officer looked me over and asked master my name, and informed me I was free, and asked me whether or not I wanted to keep living with [him]. I did not know what to do, so I told him yes. A fixed price of seventy-five dollars and board [meals] was then set as the salary I should receive per year for my work. The Yankees told me to let [them] know if I was not paid as agreed. I went back home and stayed a year. During the year I hunted a lot at night and thoroughly enjoyed being free. I took my freedom by degrees and remained obedient and respectful, but still wondering and thinking of what the future held for me. After I retired at night I made plan after plan.

Under some Black Codes passed by the Southern states, African American children like these, sitting on a porch in Hammond, Louisiana, could be taken from their parents if whites decided they were not being taken care of. The children were then made to work for white people under conditions that resembled slavery.

Robert Glenn did leave his former owner after a year, but many white Southerners did their best to keep their former slaves bound to them under new laws the Southern states passed in 1865 and 1866, known as Black Codes. Many Black Codes fined freedmen for "vagrancy" and set them to work on plantations to pay off the fines as a punishment. In Virginia, vagrants included those who would not work for "the usual and common wages given to other laborers." In South Carolina, these were "persons who lead idle or disorderly lives." In Alabama, the Black Codes said a vagrant was "a stubborn . . . servant . . . who loiters away his time." Some of the codes forbade blacks to own or lease farms or to take any jobs other than as plantation workers or domestic servants. Others allowed whites to take away the freedmen's children if they were not working. "They kept me in bondage and a girl that used to be with them," said Silas Dothrum of Arkansas, who was twelve years old in 1865. "We were bound to [our former owners so] that we would have to stay with them. . . . I wasn't allowed no kind of say-so." Millie Randall of Louisiana recalled her owners driving her and her brother Benny "round and round" in a wagon so their parents could not find them.

The Black Codes were trying to re-create slavery, if not in name, then in fact. The codes so angered U.S. lawmakers that Congress gave the Freedmen's Bureau more power in 1866. The bureau could now establish special courts for settling labor disputes, and it could cancel work agreements forced on freedmen under the codes.

The Time for Rights

In 1866, Congress also passed a civil rights bill granting African Americans protection from discrimination. President Andrew Johnson vetoed the bill—he would not sign it into law. Congress insisted and overrode his veto. The civil rights act declared that *any person* born in the United States (except American Indians) was a citizen. Then, in 1868, the Fourteenth Amendment became part of the Constitution. It further guaranteed that ex-slaves were equal citizens under the law—not property, as they had been defined in the Supreme Court's decision about Dred Scott. As citizens of the *nation*—the entire country—they could not have their rights taken away by individual state laws or by future laws that went against the Constitution. Finally, in 1870, the Fifteenth Amendment went into effect. It stated that "the right of citizens of the United States to vote shall not be denied or abridged by the United States or any State on account of race, color, or previous condition of servitude." However, this amendment broadened the right to vote for men only, not for women, black or white.

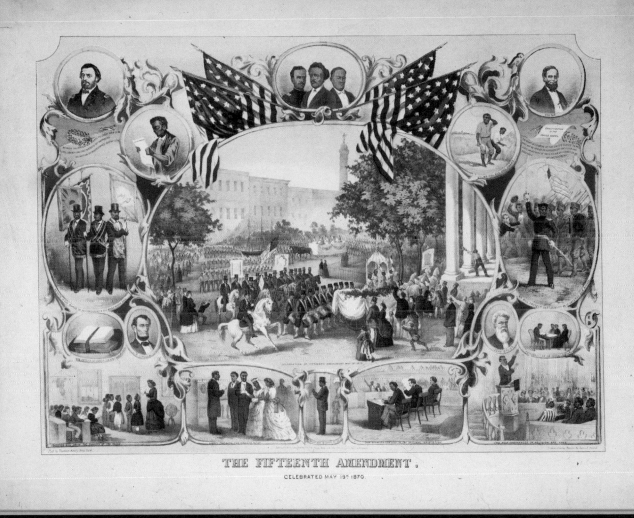

THE FIFTEENTH AMENDMENT.

CELEBRATED MAY 19ᵗʰ 1870.

In 1870, the Fifteenth Amendment granted black men the right to vote. The center of this print shows a parade in Baltimore, Maryland, celebrating the event. The other scenes show the progress of African Americans during Reconstruction, and portraits of both white and black men who contributed to the attainment of freedom.

Black and white citizens of Savannah, Georgia, vote in an outdoor square in the 1868 presidential election. A banner at the center urges people to vote for the Republican candidate, Ulysses S. Grant, who won the election.

Fifty years would pass before women were granted the right to vote in 1920 by the Nineteenth Amendment.

"The first voting I ever heard of was in Grant's election," recalled Wylie Nealy of Arkansas. Ulysses S. Grant had been the head of the Union army and was the Republican candidate for president of the United States in 1868 and 1872. The Republicans were seen as the party that had led the country through the Civil War and ended slavery. Freedmen overwhelmingly favored them. Southern Democrats, on the other hand, were associated with the Confederacy, and Democrats in the North had been more lenient toward the South in the Civil War. It was not surprising that Grant won both presidential elections.

This print, published in 1868, celebrates the new state constitution of Louisiana, written by a delegation to the constitutional convention that included African Americans. In the center is Oscar J. Dunn, Louisiana's lieutenant governor, surrounded by twenty-nine portraits of the other black delegates.

"Both black and white voted," said Nealy. "I voted Republican for Grant. . . . I was a slave for thirteen years from birth. Every slave could vote after freedom." Boston Blackwell, who was once a slave in Arkansas, also voted for Grant. "Army men came around and registered you before voting time," he said. "All you had to do was to tell who you [wanted to] vote for and they gave you a colored ticket. If you were voting for Grant, you got his color. It was easy. . . . The Constitution of the United States, it gave us the right to vote. It made us citizens, it did."

During Reconstruction, African Americans held many political offices in the U.S. Congress and in state governments, or they influenced government policies. Former slave, abolitionist, and activist Frederick Douglass, who fought for civil rights for blacks, is at the center of this print. Other contemporary and past black leaders surround him: Robert Brown Elliott (upper left), Blanche K. Bruce (upper right), and (clockwise from center top) William Wells Brown, R. T. Greener, Richard Allen, Joseph Rainey, E. D. Bassett, John Mercer Langston, P. B. S. Pinchback, and Henry Highland Garnet.

Not only could black men vote during Reconstruction, they could be elected. "There were colored men in office, plenty," said Blackwell. "Colored legislators, and colored circuit [court] clerks, and colored county clerks . . . They were all my friends." Wylie Nealy "knew several magistrates and sheriffs." African Americans served as delegates to draw up new constitutions for the Southern states. Black soldiers in the U.S. Army, representatives of the Freedmen's Bureau, black teachers and artisans and ministers, those who had been free blacks, and those who had been slaves all ran for office. Between 1869 and 1901, twenty blacks served in the U.S. House of Representatives, including Joseph Rainey of South Carolina, John Mercer Langston of Virginia, and Jefferson Long of Georgia. Two African Americans served in the Senate, both representing Mississippi: Blanche K. Bruce and Hiram Revels. Blacks also served in state legislatures and held other state offices, like Francis Cardozo, South Carolina's secretary of state, and P. B. S. Pinchback, Louisiana's lieutenant governor.

Ex-Confederates complained endlessly that they were being ruled by black Americans, but, in fact, whites kept control of state governments. During this time, no black man was ever elected governor of a Southern state, although P. B. S. Pinchback was briefly acting governor of Louisiana. Only once did blacks make up a majority of seats in a state legislature (in South Carolina), but otherwise they never controlled the laws the states passed. White Southerners were determined to keep African Americans out of government, however. Through violence, threats, tricks, and new laws, they gradually took away black men's right to vote and prevented them from holding office.

African Americans were proud of their service in the 1860s and 1870s. Black communities rallied around candidates, and black Americans gained valuable political experience. They supported important laws to allow African Americans to ride on public transportation, attend theaters, and stay at hotels, and to give everyone, black and white, an education. These laws did not always pass or stay in effect, but the effort to pass them showed a determination and commitment to equality. It was not for lack of trying that Reconstruction could not finally guarantee African Americans civil rights that were equal to those of whites, but because of politics and age-old white prejudice.

African American children attended this school in Richmond, Virginia, housed in St. Philip's Church. Harper's Weekly *printed this illustration in 1867.*

Eager to Learn

"When I was free, I went to school," recounted Mary Jane Wilson, whose father was "one of the first Negro land owners in Portsmouth [Virginia] after emancipation. . . . The first school I went to was held in a church. Soon they built a school building that was called 'Chestnut Street Academy,' and I went there. After finishing Chestnut Street Academy, I went to Hampton Institute." Hampton was one of several colleges and universities for African Americans that sprang up after the Civil War. After graduating from Hampton, Wilson became a teacher to pass on her knowledge to a new generation.

Dr. George W. Buckner, born a slave in Kentucky, got his start attending a school run by the Freedmen's Bureau. He worked as a teacher himself when he was only sixteen years old. Life was simple and rough. Buckner "boarded with an old man whose cabin was filled with his own family. I climbed a ladder leading from the cabin into a dark uncomfortable loft where a comfort[er] and a straw bed were my only conveniences." To make money, he was a waiter and worked at other odd jobs until he received more training as a teacher. Then, in 1890, he graduated from medical college and became a doctor.

Wilson and Buckner were two of the hundreds of thousands of men and women who benefited from the push to educate the freedmen. Even before the Civil War ended, Northern churches and aid societies had established schools for contrabands.

Freedwomen learn sewing skills at the Freedmen's Union Industrial School in Richmond, Virginia. This illustration appeared in Frank Leslie's Illustrated Newspaper *on September 22, 1866. Many adult freedmen and -women went to school not only to improve technical skills but to learn how to read and write.*

Classes were held in abandoned churches that whites had once attended, in cabins, in sheds, and outdoors in good weather—anywhere a group could meet. Black men and women who had been forbidden to learn to read and write under slavery flocked to lessons. In 1863, in New Bern, North Carolina, 15 of the 160 pupils were more than forty-five years old, and 95 of them were between twelve and forty-five. Black and white women and some men came from the North to teach them.

"I never before saw children so eager to learn, although I had had several years' experience in New-England schools," wrote Charlotte Forten, a black woman who herself had gone to school in Massachusetts and taught on the Sea Islands off the coast of South Carolina. "Coming to school is a constant delight and recreation to them.

Classes for African American children were held wherever room was available—cabins, churches, and outdoors, as in this photograph taken sometime after the Civil War.

The most successful achievement of Reconstruction was the increase of opportunities for education for free children, men, and women. These students learn at the "Zion" School for Colored Children in Charleston, South Carolina. This illustration, which appeared in Harper's Weekly *on December 15, 1866, was taken from a sketch by Civil War artist Alfred R. Waud.*

They come here as other children go to play. The older ones, during the summer, work in the fields from early morning until eleven or twelve o'clock, and then come into school, after their hard toil in the hot sun, so bright and as anxious to learn as ever. . . . Many of the grown people are desirous of learning to read. It is wonderful how a people who have been so long crushed to the earth . . . as they have been . . . can have so great a desire for knowledge, and such a capability for attaining it."

After the war, the Freedmen's Bureau coordinated schools set up by Northern charities. By 1869, there were nearly three thousand of them in the South, plus evening schools, private missionary schools, and schools run by individual African Americans. They made a huge difference in the lives of those who attended. Fewer than 20 percent of African Americans could read in 1870. By 1900, that number had risen to 55 percent. The advance in education was a success that would continue to grow long after Reconstruction ended.

Racism Rises: The Ku Klux Klan

Going to school, working for themselves, reuniting their families, and voting and being elected—African Americans were moving ahead during Reconstruction. But for every step forward they took, white violence tried to hold them back. Many white Southerners (and some whites in the North, too) believed in "white supremacy." This was a belief that white people were better than black people in every way. Whites should not only run the government, they should also make the rules for how African Americans lived their personal lives. Whites could not act to ensure white supremacy as openly as they did when slavery was legal, but they formed secret organizations to terrorize blacks so that they would be afraid to exercise their rights.

In the winter of 1865–1866, in Tennessee, a group of young white men started the Ku Klux Klan. At first the Klan was a social club, but soon its members began to attack schools, churches, and the homes of freedmen and whites who were sympathetic to African Americans. Singled out were teachers, Freedmen's Bureau agents, and government officials. By 1867, most Southern states had Ku Klux Klan organizations. Klan members wore disguises to hide who they were (not always successfully). They rode out at night so that darkness would cover their actions. The Klan was as powerful as the fear it could create.

"I know about the [Ku] Kluxes," said Charles Davenport of Mississippi. "They were sure enough devils walking the earth, seeking what they could devour." Lorenzo Ezell, who was a fifteen-year-old in South Carolina when the Civil War ended, remembered:

Ku Klux Klan members in a North Carolina forest plan the murder of a man named John Campbell. Frank Leslie's Illustrated Newspaper *printed this illustration on October 7, 1871.*

We left the plantation in [18]65 or '66 and by '68 we were having such an awful time with the [Ku] Klux. [The] first time they came to my mamma's house at midnight and claimed they [were] soldiers . . . come back from the dead. They [were] all dressed up in sheets and made up like spirits. They groaned around and said they [had] been killed wrongly and come back for justice. . . . My mamma never did take up no truck with spirits so she knew it was just a man. They told us what they [were going] to do if we didn't all go back to our masters and we all agreed and they all disappeared.

After Ezell and his family moved to New Prospect, South Carolina:

'TWO MEMBERS OF THE KU-KLUX KLAN IN THEIR DISGUISES.'

The second swarm of the [Ku] Klux came out. They claimed they [were going to] kill everybody who was Republican. My daddy [was] charged with being a leader amongst the [black people]. He made a speech and instructed the [blacks] how to vote for Grant. . . . The [Ku] Klux wanted to whip him and he had to sleep in a hollow log every night. . . . The funny thing [is], I knew all those [Ku] Klux despite their sheets. . . . I knew their voices and their saddle horses.

Other secret societies like the Klan sprang up throughout the South. Louisiana had the Knights of the White Camellia; Texas, the Knights of the Rising Sun; Mississippi, the White Line. These were terrorist groups, shooting off weapons, burning buildings, threatening lives, and sometimes killing those who championed the rights of freedmen. If a black man voted, like Lorenzo Ezell's father, he was a target; if he owned land or wanted to buy more, he was a target. Black soldiers of the U.S. Army, stationed in the South after the Civil War, were prime targets.

White supremacists wanted to regain full control of the South and to re-create, as much as possible, the world of slavery. They wanted to control black labor and black lives. Their greatest weapon was fear. Elections in the South could not be fair as long as African Americans were too frightened to vote. Even if they were not murdered, they could lose their jobs or be evicted from their land for speaking out.

Violence was so widespread that the U.S. Congress had to do something. In 1870 and 1871, it passed two laws called Enforcement Acts, which would fine or imprison anyone trying to stop African American men from voting. Interfering in an election became a national, not a state crime. A third Enforcement Act—called the Ku Klux Klan Act—said that the U.S. government could use military force if any state, or group within a state, denied blacks their rights. These laws were difficult to enforce—witnesses of Klan and other violence were often afraid to testify. But violence decreased for a while. The national presidential election and state elections in 1872 were the most fair and peaceful ones the South had ever had or would have for decades to come.

OPPOSITE *Members of the Ku Klux Klan disguised themselves when they terrorized African Americans in the Southern states. This illustration appeared in* Harper's Weekly *on December 19, 1868.*

HARPER'S WEEKLY.

A JOURNAL OF CIVILIZATION.

VOL. X.—No. 491.]   NEW YORK, SATURDAY, MAY 26, 1866.   [SINGLE COPIES TEN CENTS. $4.00 PER YEAR IN ADVANCE.

Entered according to Act of Congress, in the Year 1866, by Harper & Brothers, in the Clerk's Office of the District Court for the Southern District of New York.

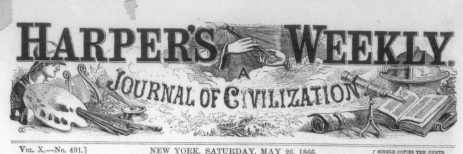

THE MEMPHIS RIOTS.

THERE was in Memphis, on the first two days of May, an excitement unequaled since the close of the war. The origin of the disturbance between the whites and negroes of that city was highly discreditable to the colored soldiers, and the riotous proceedings which followed were a disgrace to civilization. For the riot the lower class of white citizens were as responsible as were the soldiers of the Third United States Colored Infantry for the original difficulty. This regiment, whose reputation has been a bad one, had been mustered out, since which they had frequented whisky-shops in the southern part of the city, and had been guilty of excesses and disorderly conduct. On the evening of May 1 some drunken members of the regiment were on South Street, talking noisily, when in an insolent manner they were ordered by two policemen to cease their noise and disperse. Words ensued, followed by blows, throwing of missiles, and firing of revolvers.

To understand what followed it must be remembered that the police force of Memphis is composed mostly of Irishmen, whose violent prejudice against negroes was as shamefully displayed in the New York riots of 1863. The *Times* correspondent thus described the riot:

Word was sent to police head-quarters, and the whole force at once proceeded to the scene of the fray, being joined on the way thither by armed and excited citizens. Meanwhile the firing had brought other negroes to the spot, some armed with clubs and some with revolvers, so that by the time the police force came up the two parties were about equal in number. The negroes held the original

position, and, upon the approach of the police, showing no determination to abandon it, were fired upon by the police and citizens who accompanied them. This fire was returned, and for a while both parties busied themselves in discharging their revolvers as rapidly as possible. Meanwhile word was sent to General STONEMAN, who promptly dispatched to the scene of action a company of Regulars (white), when the negroes were quickly dispersed and driven in every direction.

During the evening the wildest and most exaggerated reports were spread throughout the city. Every communicator of the intelligence of the fight told a different story, and the highest excitement prevailed. Each rumor placed a worse aspect upon the affair than the preceding one, and only served to develop the pent-up prejudice against the negro. Soon after dark this excitement and prejudice found vent. Large numbers of armed citizens repaired to the scene of the fight and commenced firing upon every negro who made himself visible. One negro upon South Street, a quiet, inoffensive laborer, was shot down almost in front of his own cabin, and after life was extinct his body was fired into, cut and beat in a most horrible manner. In all parts of the city, wherever they could be seen, negroes were fired upon by policemen as well as citizens. They were shot while driving horks, and quietly walking in the streets about their business. The police seemed to make it their special business to shoot every negro they could see, no matter where he was or what he was doing. The result was that by 9 o'clock the colored population were in-doors trembling with wild alarm. How many negroes were killed during the night it is impossible to ascertain, as firing was constantly heard during the earlier hours in all parts of the city. It is estimated that from 15 to 20 were killed. So far as I have been able to learn, not a white man was fired upon by a negro during the whole night.

After the fight of Tuesday evening the negro soldiers and most of the colored population residing in the vicinity of the fight fled to the fort for security. They were perfectly quiet—in fact, were terribly frightened for their own safety. At an early hour yesterday morning every thing

SCENES IN MEMPHIS, TENNESSEE, DURING THE RIOT—BURNING A FREEDMEN'S SCHOOL-HOUSE.

[SKETCHED BY A. R. W.]

SCENES IN MEMPHIS, TENNESSEE, DURING THE RIOT—SHOOTING DOWN NEGROES ON THE MORNING OF MAY 2, 1866.—[SKETCHED BY A. R. W.]

This print of President Ulysses S. Grant (left, at table) signing the Ku Klux Klan Act in the Capitol Building ran in Frank Leslie's Illustrated Newspaper *on May 13, 1871. The act allowed the federal government to use military force in protecting civil and political rights.*

Reconstruction Ends

The North's victory in the Civil War ended slavery and carried the promise of a new life for black Americans. In the 1860s and early 1870s, some freedmen did come to own their own land, and many went to school, exercised political rights, and experienced the first taste of liberty. But the freedom and equality enjoyed by African Americans always depended on the United States government to pass laws that would support them. Sometimes the government succeeded, and sometimes it failed.

Those Southerners who had supported the Confederacy, who had supported slavery, and who still supported white supremacy did not give up because the war came to an end. Racial prejudice still lived in the hearts of many white Southerners as well as Northern whites. Many Southern states resisted the laws that made elections fair or protected blacks in their homes, work, and schools. Northerners, in turn, lost the will to enforce these laws. The number of U.S. soldiers stationed in the South to make sure elections were fair grew smaller and smaller. Northerners became tired of interceding to stop violence in the South. They no longer wanted to fight against other white men and women. In 1873, there was an economic depression, and people throughout the United States were poorer and jobs were harder to find. The U.S. government no longer focused on the Southern states; it turned its attention to ways to make the economy better in the North and West. The feeling grew that Southern whites (although many had been Confederate leaders) knew best how to govern the South now.

In 1875, Congress did pass another civil rights bill, but it was a weak one. African Americans would have to prove discrimination in a court of law. They would have to make the claim themselves, rather than have representatives of the federal government make it on their behalf. The overscheduled courts took a long time to bring a case to trial. Then, while campaigning for the presidency in 1876, Rutherford B. Hayes said that he would restore "the blessings of honest and capable local self-government to the South" if he were elected. Hayes was a Republican, from the same political party as Abraham Lincoln and Ulysses S. Grant. Yet the "local self-government" he supported was, in fact, rule by whites only.

Hayes ran against Democrat Samuel Tilden, the choice of most whites in the South. When the votes were counted, it was uncertain who had won the presidency. In Louisiana, South Carolina, and Florida it was also not clear who had been elected governor. The Republicans claimed victory and so did the Democrats, who were former Confederates. Two governments formed in these states, each threatening to eliminate the other, even by force. It seemed possible that war would break out in South Carolina and Louisiana. U.S. government soldiers were called out to protect the Republican candidates.

No one, in the North or the South, really wanted another war so soon after the Civil War had ended. Again, as in 1820 and 1850, a compromise was worked out. The Republican Hayes became president of the United States. The Democrats became the governors in Louisiana and South Carolina. Hayes withdrew the small number of U.S. forces who had been guarding state government buildings to keep the Republicans safe in these states. As part of the deal, there were also compromises about economic aid and political positions.

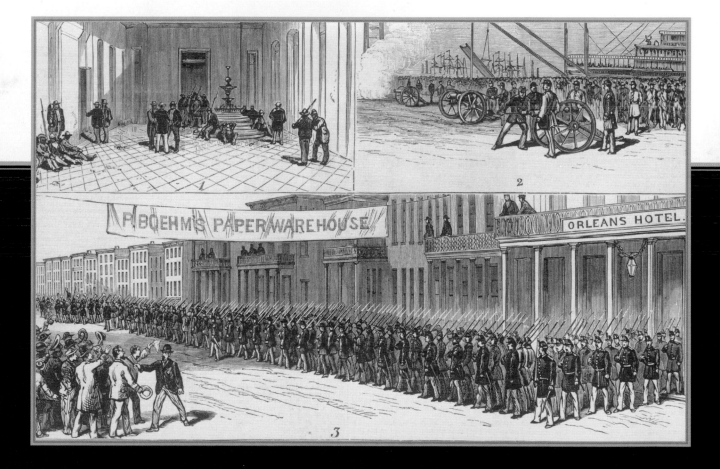

Frank Leslie's Illustrated Newspaper *of May 19, 1877, printed these sketches of the activities on the day that U.S. soldiers were ordered to stop guarding the statehouse in New Orleans, Louisiana. One sketch (top, left) shows the inner courtyard of the statehouse, another (top, right) shows a cannon salute to celebrate the end of the building's evacuation, and the bottom sketch shows the soldiers heading back to their barracks.*

RIGHT *This print, published in 1883, six years after Reconstruction ended, shows the "Sunny South," where African Americans peacefully pick cotton by the side of the Mississippi River. This picture depicts life in the South the way many white Americans thought it should be or wanted it to be. It does not convey the reality of black life that included violence, poverty, and the loss of civil and political rights.*

OPPOSITE *Despite the setback of rights and opportunities for African Americans after 1877, education continued to be important. Many schools for black children lacked nice buildings and equipment, but some were models for how future learning could take place. This photograph shows a teacher and students at the Annie Davis School near Tuskegee, Alabama. It was taken circa 1902 by photographer Frances Benjamin Johnston.*

But for African Americans, the compromises of 1877 meant that the Southern states could freely move ahead to eliminate their rights, limit their ability to make a living, and discriminate against them in schools and in public places. A system of segregation—complete separation—of blacks and whites hardened into place. By 1900, segregation laws kept most blacks in separate housing and schools and locked into low-paying jobs, without protection from discrimination and violence. African Americans lost the civil and political rights they had exercised briefly in the 1860s and 1870s. Not until the civil rights movement of the 1950s and 1960s would the U.S. government again take an active role in protecting the rights of black Americans.

A Freedwoman Looks Back and to the Future

Would the story of Reconstruction end so sadly? Would the faith that once-enslaved men and women had in a better life be disappointed? In 1902, Susie King Taylor, a fugitive slave who worked as a laundress and teacher with a black regiment during the Civil War, recounted what she saw happening to African Americans in the United States. "Living here in Boston where the black man is given equal justice, I must say a word on the general treatment of my race, both in the North and South, in the twentieth century," wrote Taylor.

I wonder if our white fellow men realize the true sense of meaning of brotherhood? For two hundred years we had toiled for them; the war of 1861 came and was ended, and we thought our race was forever freed from bondage, and that the two races could live in unity with each other, but when we read almost every day of what is being done to my race by some whites in the South, I sometimes ask, "Was the war in vain? Has it brought freedom, in the full sense of the word, or has it made our condition more hopeless? . . .

There are still good friends to the negro. Why, there are still thousands. . . . Man thinks two hundred years is a long time, and it is, too; but it is only as a week to God, and in his own time . . . the South will be like the North, and when it comes it will be prized higher than we prize the North to-day. God is just; when he created man he made him in his image, and never intended one should misuse the other. All men are born free and equal in his sight.

African Americans continued to believe this, even in the hard times. They lost many of their rights, but they had gained something in Reconstruction: a sense of dignity and worth, a sense of purpose. They would not be silenced; they persisted in being heard. They thrived in school, they established churches, they formed families, they came together in communities. They depended on each other, and they built their own strengths. They stored up pride, determination, and courage to get them through the difficult years of the first half of the twentieth century. They used the years after the Civil War, the Reconstruction years, to understand what freedom meant and to always hold it dear.

Taken between 1880 and 1890, this photograph suggests the progress African Americans made after the Civil War, no matter what obstacles were placed in their way. This prosperous and handsome group looks toward a future of hope, pride, and achievement.

Time Line

1619
+ The first Africans land in the English colonies that will become the United States.

1663
+ The colony of Maryland passes a law that declares "all negroes and other slaves" be enslaved for their entire lifetime and that the children of slaves shall also be enslaved.

1759
+ Anthony Benezet, a white Quaker and early abolitionist in Pennsylvania, publishes his first anti-slavery pamphlet.

1776
+ American colonists write and sign the Declaration of Independence, proclaiming their independence from Britain and stating that "all men are created equal."

1777
+ Vermont's constitution prohibits slavery.

1787
+ The United States Constitution, the foundation for all U.S. laws, is written. It does not prohibit slavery.

1793
+ Eli Whitney invents the cotton gin. This machine quickly separates cotton fibers from the seed, so that cotton farming becomes very profitable.

1803
+ The United States buys the Louisiana Purchase from France, enormously increasing America's territory.

1808
+ The United States bans the foreign slave trade, as indicated in the Constitution. Slaves can no longer be brought to the United States from Africa.

1816
+ The American Colonization Society is founded to send free blacks back to Africa. Few black Americans want to go.

1820
+ Under the Missouri Compromise, Congress agrees to let Missouri join the Union as a slave state and Maine to join as a free state. Slavery will not be allowed in the northern part of the Louisiana Territory, above the 36° 30' parallel on a map.

1829
+ David Walker, a free African American, writes his *Appeal*, calling for slaves to rebel. The Southern states forbid anyone to distribute it to the public.

1831
+ William Lloyd Garrison begins publication of *The Liberator*, an abolitionist newspaper.

1833
+ The American Anti-Slavery Society is founded.

1840
+ The Liberty Party, the first political party to support abolition, runs James G. Birney as a candidate for president. He gets less than 1 percent of the vote.

1845
+ Frederick Douglass publishes the first edition of his *Narrative*, telling stories of his experiences as a slave.

1846
+ The Mexican War begins after the United States claims Texas, which had declared its independence from Mexico, as a slave state. When the war ends in 1848, the United States receives land as part of the Treaty of Guadalupe Hidalgo with Mexico and buys additional land as the Gadsden Purchase. These territories will become the states of California, Utah, Nevada, and Arizona, and parts of New Mexico, Colorado, and Wyoming.

1848
+ The Free Soil Party, a political party that believes there should be no slavery in the territories, wins thirteen seats in the House of Representatives and one seat in the Senate.

1849
+ Harriet Tubman escapes from slavery.

1850
+ Several laws are passed that make up the Compromise of 1850. California enters the Union as a free state, but citizens living in the rest of the territory acquired from Mexico may choose whether their states will be slave states. The Fugitive Slave Law requires free states to return runaway slaves to their owners.

1854
+ Runaway slave Anthony Burns is arrested in Boston under the Fugitive Slave Law. Despite strong protests by abolitionists, he is returned to his owner at great cost to the federal government.

+ Congress passes the Kansas-Nebraska Act, which repeals (takes back) the part of the Missouri Compromise that forbade slavery in the northern part of the territory. Under the new law, settlers in the territories of Kansas and Nebraska can decide for themselves whether their territories will allow slavery. Much violence between pro-slavery and anti-slavery settlers and their supporters will follow.

+ The Republican Party is founded. It calls for repeal of the Kansas-Nebraska Act and the Fugitive Slave Law. The party is against the spread of slavery to new territories.

1857
+ The United States Supreme Court rules in *Scott v. Sanford* that Dred Scott, a slave who sued in a U.S. court for his freedom, had no right to sue because as a slave he was not a U.S. citizen, but property.

1859
+ Abolitionist John Brown and twenty-one others take over the United States arsenal at Harpers Ferry, Virginia (now in West Virginia). They hope that slaves will rebel using the weapons, but Brown and his followers are captured by U.S. government soldiers instead.

1860
+ Abraham Lincoln of the Republican Party is elected president of the United States.

+ South Carolina secedes from the Union.

1861
+ Florida, Alabama, Georgia, Mississippi, and Louisiana secede from the Union in January. Texas secedes in February. The states that secede in January, and South Carolina, form a new country, the Confederate States of America. Texas will soon join the Confederacy.

+ South Carolinian soldiers shell Fort Sumter, a U.S. fort in Charleston, South Carolina, Harbor. U.S. soldiers surrender. Lincoln calls for troops to fight back. The Civil War begins.

+ Virginia, Arkansas, and Tennessee secede from the Union.

+ Union general Benjamin Butler calls runaway slaves who reach Union lines "contraband of war." He refuses to return them to their owners. This will become Union policy.

+ Congress passes the First Confiscation Act, which states that contrabands who had been working directly for the Confederate army will not be returned.

+ Mary Chase opens the first school for contrabands, in Alexandria, Virginia.

1862
+ Jefferson Davis is inaugurated as president of the Confederate States.

+ President Abraham Lincoln signs into law a bill banning slavery in U.S. territories. Congress passes the Second Confiscation Act, which calls for freedom for all slaves owned by people who support the Confederacy.

+ President Lincoln issues the Preliminary Emancipation Proclamation, declaring that slaves in the Confederate States will be freed on January 1, 1863.

1863
+ President Lincoln issues the Emancipation Proclamation, freeing the slaves in the Confederate States and allowing African American men to enlist in the Union army.

+ The Confederate Congress gives Jefferson Davis the authority to "put to death" black soldiers taken as prisoners of war. The Union objects to this ruling.

- A battle between Union and Confederate forces takes place at Gettysburg, Pennsylvania, the only large battle fought in a Union state. The Confederate soldiers are forced to retreat.

- The Fifty-Fourth Massachusetts Colored Regiment storms the Confederate Fort Wagner, in Charleston, South Carolina, Harbor. Many are killed, and they fail to take the fort, but word spreads of black Americans' bravery in battle.

- Frederick Douglass meets with President Lincoln, protesting the fact that black soldiers in the Union army are paid less than white soldiers.

1864

- African Americans from New Orleans, Louisiana, present a petition with more than one thousand signatures to President Lincoln, calling for the right to vote. Lincoln writes to the Union governor of Louisiana, instructing him that, when a new state constitution is written, the state should consider giving the vote to black men who are educated, own land, or served in the Union army.

- The U.S. Congress passes a law granting equal pay to black and white soldiers.

- In Syracuse, New York, 144 African Americans from eighteen states (including seven slave states) meet for a national black convention and organize a National Equal Rights League.

- Abraham Lincoln is reelected president of the United States.

1865

- Union major general William T. Sherman orders that black Americans have their own land on the coast between South Carolina and Florida. More than forty thousand freedmen will settle this land, but they will be evicted when President Andrew Johnson withdraws the order.

- The Thirteenth Amendment, forbidding slavery in the United States, becomes part of the Constitution.

- Congress creates the Freedmen's Bureau to assist former slaves.

- The Confederate States surrender to the Union, ending the Civil War.

- Abraham Lincoln is assassinated by a Southern sympathizer, John Wilkes Booth.

- Andrew Johnson becomes the U.S. president. He pardons most Confederates if they take an oath of loyalty to the United States.

- Southern states begin passing Black Codes, restricting the rights of the freedmen.

1866

- The Ku Klux Klan is formed in Tennessee.

- Congress passes the first civil rights bill over a veto by President Johnson.

- Tennessee becomes the first Confederate state readmitted to the Union.

1867

- Congress gives the right to vote to black Americans in Washington, D.C.

- The Radical Republicans in Congress pass three Reconstruction Acts over President Johnson's veto. The first Reconstruction Act organizes the former Confederacy into five military districts, which are run by the U.S. Army to keep peace and ensure the safety of the freedmen. The second and third acts give details of how this plan will work.

1868

- A fourth Reconstruction Act becomes law. It allows the Southern states to ratify new state constitutions based on the number of people who actually vote.

- Arkansas, Alabama, Florida, Louisiana, North Carolina, and South Carolina are readmitted to the Union.

- The Fourteenth Amendment, declaring African Americans to be citizens, becomes part of the Constitution.

- Ulysses S. Grant is elected president of the United States.

1869

- Democrats, many of whom had supported the Confederacy, are elected and take over the state legislature of Tennessee.

1870

- Virginia, Georgia, Mississippi, and Texas are readmitted to the Union.

- Hiram Revels, the first African American elected to the U.S. Senate, takes the seat once held by Jefferson Davis in Congress. He represents Mississippi.

- The Fifteenth Amendment, granting black men the right to vote, becomes part of the Constitution.

- Joseph H. Rainey, the first African American elected to the U.S. House of Representatives, is seated in Congress.

1871

- Congress passes the Ku Klux Klan Act to help stop violence against the freedmen and their white supporters in the South.

- Democrats, many of them former Confederates, take over the state legislature of Georgia.

1872

- Frederick Douglass leads a national gathering of African Americans in New Orleans. This convention seeks guaranteed political and civil rights for African Americans.

- Ulysses S. Grant is reelected president of the United States.

1873

- Despite the Ku Klux Klan Act, violence continues against African Americans and their white supporters in the South.

- A serious economic depression causes concern throughout the United States.

1874

- President Grant refuses to send U.S. troops to keep Republican governor Edmund Davis of Texas in power. A Democrat replaces him.

- Democrats take over the governorship and legislature of Alabama.

- A Democrat is elected governor of Arkansas.

1875

- President Grant signs the second Civil Rights Act into law, granting all Americans access to public hotels, theaters, and other buildings. It will be weakly enforced.

- Democrats win control of the Mississippi legislature.

1876

- The results of the presidential election between Republican Rutherford B. Hayes and Democrat Samuel Tilden are in dispute. State elections for governors in Florida, South Carolina, and Louisiana are also disputed.

1877

- The Democratic candidate, George F. Drew, is inaugurated as governor of Florida.

- Rutherford B. Hayes is declared president of the United States after negotiations with Southern Democrats.

- U.S. soldiers are withdrawn from the statehouses in Louisiana and South Carolina. A Democratic governor takes over Louisiana, and Wade Hampton, a Democrat who had been a Confederate general, begins his term as governor of South Carolina.

After Reconstruction ended, in the later part of the nineteenth century, the states of the former Confederacy passed segregation laws separating black and white Americans in schools, public places, on buses and railroads, and in most activities of daily life. In some parts of Northern and Western states there was also legal segregation; but the majority of African Americans living in the North and West were separated from whites because of discrimination (unfair treatment), not laws. Discrimination grew out of custom, economics, politics, and especially racial prejudice.

In 1896, the Supreme Court ruled in *Plessy v. Ferguson* that transportation and facilities could be separate as long as they were equal. In fact, segregation almost never provided equal accommodations for African Americans. In 1909, blacks and whites founded the National Association for the Advancement of Colored People (NAACP) to fight against segregation and racial discrimination. In 1954, the Supreme Court reversed the *Plessy* decision in *Brown v. Board of Education*, declaring that separate schools were by their nature unequal and calling for school integration. This was an important step in the civil rights movement of the 1950s and 1960s. In 1963, the March on Washington led to the passage the following year of a civil rights law making segregation illegal. In 1965, one hundred years after the Civil War ended, Congress passed a law outlawing discriminatory practices used to prevent African Americans from voting.

119

Page 7: "Sometimes I think . . . give up our lives for it." Marietta Hill, manuscript pages, Myrtilla Miner Papers, Container 1, "Essays and Drawings by Students (1852–1854)," Library of Congress Manuscript Division.

Page 13: "See your declaration, Americans!! . . . your own language." Quoted in David Walker, *Walker's Appeal, with a Brief Sketch of His Life*, ed. Henry Highland Garnet (New York: J.H. Tobitt, 1848), p. 85.

Page 13: "A house divided . . . cannot stand." Abraham Lincoln, in a speech from June 1858. http://www.nationalcenter.org/HouseDivided.html (accessed August 22, 2008).

Page 15: On Emily and Mary Edmonson. Mary Kay Ricks, *Escape on the Pearl: The Heroic Bid for Freedom on the Underground Railroad* (New York: William Morrow, 2007).

Page 18: "[N]o male person, born in this country . . . bound by their own consent . . ." Constitution of the State of Vermont, http://www.yale.edu/lawweb/avalon/states/vt01.htm (accessed June 11, 2008).

Page 18: "one day, when all our people . . . into the nearest wood." Olaudah Equiano, *The Interesting Narrative of the Life of Olaudah Equiano, or Gustavas Vassa, the African* (1789), in *Slave Narratives*, eds. William L. Andrews and Henry Louis Gates Jr. (New York: Library of America, 2000), p. 66.

Pages 22–23: "I remember a man named Rough . . . to those slave sales." Cornelia Andrews, Federal Writers' Project interview, in *North Carolina Slave Narratives* (Bedford, MA: Applewood Books; Washington, D.C.: Library of Congress, Print on Demand), pp. 28–29. Lightly edited for readability for all ages.

Page 23: "whipped in public . . . being slow." Ibid., p. 29. Lightly edited for readability for all ages.

Page 24: "Come daybreak . . . by the bells and horns!" Charley Williams, Federal Writers' Project interview, in *Remembering Slavery: African Americans Talk about Their Personal Experiences of Slavery and Emancipation*, eds. Ira Berlin et al. (New York: The New Press, 1998), pp. 84–85. Lightly edited for readability for all ages.

Page 26: "lay from the opening o' spring . . . dare you to cry.'" James Abbot, Federal Writers' Project interview, in *Missouri Slave Narratives* (Bedford, MA: Applewood Books; Washington, D.C.: Library of Congress, Print on Demand), p. 1. Lightly edited for readability for all ages.

Page 26: "Lord! I've seen such brutish doings . . . wiggle and holler." Lucretia Alexander, Federal Writers' Project interview, in *Arkansas Slave Narratives* (Bedford, MA: Applewood Books; Washington, D.C.: Library of Congress, Print on Demand), p. 34. Lightly edited for readability for all ages.

Page 28: "overseer beat . . . their heels." David Blont, Federal Writers' Project interview, in *Voices from Slavery: 100 Authentic Slave Narratives*, ed. Norman Yetman (Mineola, NY: Dover Publications, 2000), p. 30. Lightly edited for readability for all ages.

Pages 28–29: "I 'member one time . . . across the floor." David Blont, Federal Writers' Project interview, in *Missouri Slave Narratives*, p. 3. Lightly edited for readability for all ages.

Page 29: "[My] lessons in reading . . . became [my] blackboard." Frederick Douglass, manuscript page of autobiographical article for *The National Cyclopaedia of American Biography*, Frederick Douglass Papers, Library of Congress Manuscript Division.

Pages 30–31: "Babies were snatched . . . own you soul and body." Delia Garlic, Federal Writers' Project interview, in *Remembering Slavery*, eds. Berlin et al., p. 8. Lightly edited for readability for all ages.

Page 31: "I was taken away . . . by day and by night." Henry Bibb, *Narrative of the Life and Adventures of Henry Bibb, An American Slave* (1849), in *Slave Narratives*, eds. Andrews and Gates, p. 442.

Pages 33–34: "a week had passed . . . bite was poisonous." Harriet Jacobs, *Incidents in the Life of a Slave Girl: Written by Herself* (1861), ed. Nell Irvin Painter. (New York: Penguin, 2000), p. 110.

Page 34: "The rats and mice . . . an intolerable burning." Ibid., pp. 128, 130.

Page 35: "to go out to the fields . . . the plantation overseer." Aaron Griggs, quoted in Deborah Gray White, *Let My People Go: African Americans 1804–1860* (New York: Oxford University Press, 1996), p. 79.

Page 35: free blacks . . . a few even owning slaves themselves. Some free blacks in the slave states owned slaves themselves. In New Orleans, for example, more than three thousand free blacks were slave owners. See Eric Foner, *Reconstruction: America's Unfinished Revolution 1863–1877* (New York: Harper & Row, 1989), p. 47, and http://americancivilwar.com/authors/black_slaveowners.htm (accessed June 10, 2008).

Page 38: "How bright and beautiful . . . walk by the water." Charlotte Forten, quoted in *A Free Black Girl Before the Civil War: The Diary of Charlotte Forten, 1854*, eds. Christy Steele and Kerry Graves (Mankato, MN: Blue Earth Books, 2000), p. 8.

Page 38: "How strange . . . suffering in chains." Ibid., p. 16

Page 39: "was far from being . . . against it." Charles C. Andrews, *The History of New-York African Free-Schools* (New York: M. Day, 1830), p. 16.

Page 39: "reading . . . astronomy." Ibid., p. 62

Page 39: "of which number . . . suspenders &c. 42." Ibid., p. 43.

Page 39: "On Freedom." Ibid., p. 65.

Page 40 (caption): "Are all the children . . . Alas for them!" *The Child's Anti-Slavery Book: Containing a Few Words about American Slave Children and Stories of Slave-Life* (New York: Carlton & Porter, 1860), p. 10.

Page 41: "Remember one great truth . . . to his heirs forever." Ibid., pp. 13–15.

Page 45: "The masses of . . . worth living in." John Rock, quoted in James M. McPherson, *The Negro's Civil War: How American Blacks Felt and Acted During the War for the Union* (New York: Vintage Books, 2003), p. 83.

Pages 45–46: "We are Americans . . . will become more so." Frederick Douglass, quoted in Ibid., p. 84.

Page 47: "Our work will not be done . . . some of our white voters." Frederick Douglass, quoted in Ibid., p. 275.

Page 47: "We contend . . . which we live." Kansas African Americans, quoted in Ibid., pp. 278–279.

Pages 50–51: On Anthony Burns. *Dictionary of American Negro Biography*, eds. Rayford W. Logan and Michael R. Winston (New York: W.W. Norton, 1982), pp. 80–81.

Page 53: "This Court acknowledges too . . . no wrong, but RIGHT." John Brown, quoted in *The African American Odyssey*, ed. Deborah Newman Ham (Washington, D.C.: Library of Congress, 1998), p. 22.

Page 53 (caption): "altogether unfit . . . bound to respect." Roger Taney, quoted in Paul Finkelman, *Slavery in the Courtroom* (Washington, D.C.: Library of Congress, 1985), p. 48.

Page 54: "I sometimes think . . . give up our lives for it?" See note for page 7.

Page 57: "Just before the war . . . the South to win." William Adams, Federal Writers' Project interview, in *Remembering Slavery*, eds. Berlin et al., p. 213. Lightly edited for readability for all ages.

Page 58: "foundations are laid . . . normal condition." Alexander Stephens, quoted in *The Library of Congress Civil War Desk Reference*, eds. Margaret Wagner et al. (New York: Simon & Schuster, 2002), p. 68.

Page 59: "Next thing we knew . . . the Yankees [Union soldiers] did later on." Isaac Adams, Federal Writers' Project interview, in *Remembering Slavery*, eds. Berlin et al., p. 231. Lightly edited for readability for all ages.

Page 60: "I have seen . . . people were dogs." Cato Carter, Federal Writers' Project interview, in *Remembering Slavery*, eds. Berlin et al., p. 261. Lightly edited for readability for all ages.

Pages 60–61: "One day a man . . . I wouldn't get hurt." Rachel Cruze, Federal Writers' Project interview, in *Remembering Slavery*, eds. Berlin et al., p. 253. Lightly edited for readability for all ages.

Page 61: "Those cannons . . . red with the slaughter." Ibid., pp. 253–254. Lightly edited for readability for all ages.

Page 62: "dressing me in the dark . . . we get along pretty good." Mary Barbour, Federal Writers' Project interview, in *North Carolina Slave Narratives*, pp. 79–81. Lightly edited for readability for all ages.

Page 64: "half scared to death." John Finnely, Federal Writers' Project interview, in *Remembering Slavery*, eds. Berlin et al., p. 219. Lightly edited for readability for all ages.

Page 64: "The noise was awful . . . any such again." Ibid, pp. 219–220. Lightly edited for readability for all ages.

Page 65: "I've never been to school . . . the lesson." Lorenzo Ezell, Federal Writers' Project interview, in *Voices from Slavery*, ed. Yetman, p. 115. Lightly edited for readability for all ages.

Pages 65–66: "to help clear roads . . . cut roads through timber." Thomas Cole, Federal Writers' Project interview, in *Remembering Slavery*, eds. Berlin et al., pp. 226–227. Lightly edited for readability for all ages.

Pages 66–67: "Now, therefore I, Abraham Lincoln . . . freedom of said persons." Emancipation Proclamation, http://www.archives.gov/exhibits/featured_documents/emancipation_proclamation (accessed May 14, 2008).

Pages 67–69: "Seeing such a multitude . . . seen again in this life." Henry M. Turner, quoted in McPherson, *The Negro's Civil War*, pp. 49–50.

Page 70: "Please tell these little people . . . wills to do it." Abraham Lincoln, in a letter responding to a "Children's Petition to the president asking him to free all the little slave children in this country," 1864. Quoted in http://news.yahoo.com/s/afp/20080403/ts_alt_afp/ushistorypoliticsauctionlincoln (accessed April 3, 2008).

Page 72: "We can remember . . . our natural manhood." Thomas Long, quoted in Leon F. Litwack, *Been in the Storm So Long: The Aftermath of Slavery* (New York: Knopf, 1979), p. 102. Lightly edited for readability for all ages.

Page 73: "The Yankees burned Hampton . . . than anything I know." Richard Slaughter, Federal Writers' Project interview, in *Virginia Slave Narratives* (Bedford, MA: Applewood Books; Washington, D.C.: Library of Congress, Print on Demand), pp. 46–47. Lightly edited for readability for all ages.

Page 74: "about seventeen years old . . . off my back, I guess." Ibid., pp. 47–48. Lightly edited for readability for all ages.

Page 74: "Why are we not worth . . . to impose upon us." African American soldier, quoted in McPherson, *The Negro's Civil War*, pp. 202–203.

Page 75: "It is no longer . . . the colored race." *The New York Times*, quoted in Ibid., p. 189.

Pages 76–77: "Not a man flinched . . . an end to this war." Lewis Douglass, quoted in Ibid., pp. 194–195.

Page 77: "Words would fail to describe . . . on every side." Charles Fox, quoted in Ibid., p. 240.

Page 79: "Talk about hard times! . . . house for seasoning." Andrew Moss, Federal Writers' Project interview, in *Voices from Slavery*, ed. Yetman, p. 233. Lightly edited for readability for all ages.

Pages 83–84: On the number of U.S. soldiers stationed in the South after the Civil War. James E. Sefton, *The United States Army and Reconstruction 1865–1877* (Baton Rouge: Louisiana State Press, 1967), pp. 260–262.

Pages 86–87: "One day I was out . . . it's happy." Tom Robinson, Federal Writers' Project interview, in *Voices from Slavery*, ed. Yetman, p. 255. Lightly edited for readability for all ages.

Page 88: "I reckon I was glad . . . family [had been] sold." Charlie Barbour, Federal Writers' Project interview, in *North Carolina Slave Narratives*, p. 76. Lightly edited for readability for all ages.

Page 88: "They had a passion . . . were reunited." John DeForest, quoted in Litwack, *Been in the Storm So Long*, p. 230.

Page 89: "Glory! Glory! Hallelujah! . . . you were alive." Ben Dodson, quoted in Ibid., p. 229. Lightly edited for readability for all ages.

Page 89: "Information Wanted . . . Lucinda Lowery, Nashville." Ibid, p. 232.

Page 90: "to do cooking . . . required of her." Contract for employment, quoted in Noralee Frankel, *Break Those Chains at Last: African Americans 1860–1880* (New York: Oxford University Press, 1996), p. 82.

Page 90: "The property . . . of our brows." A freedman, quoted in Ibid., p. 79.

Pages 90–91: "We have a right . . . divine right to the land." A freedman, quoted in Ibid., p. 79. Lightly edited for readability for all ages.

Pages 91–92: "Well, now, they tell me . . . after surrender." Isom Mosely, Federal Writers' Project interview, in *Remembering Slavery*, eds. Berlin et al., p. 323. Lightly edited for readability for all ages.

Page 94: "Master told me . . . plan after plan." Robert Glenn, Federal Writers' Project interview, in *Voices from Slavery*, ed. Yetman, p. 138. Lightly edited for readability for all ages.

Page 95: "the usual . . . laborers." From Virginia black code, quoted in *The Library of Congress Civil War Desk Reference*, eds. Wagner et al., p. 766.

Page 95: "persons . . . disorderly lives." From South Carolina black code, quoted in Ibid., p. 766.

Pages 95: "a stubborn . . . his time." From Alabama black code, quoted in Ibid., p. 766.

Page 96: "They kept me . . . say-so." Silas Dothrum, quoted in Litwack, *Been in the Storm So Long*, p. 191.

Page 96: "round and round." Millie Randall, quoted in Ibid., p. 191.

Page 98: "The first voting . . . election." Wylie Nealy, Federal Writers' Project interview, in *Voices from Slavery*, ed. Yetman, p. 235. Lightly edited for readability for all ages.

Page 99: "Both black and white . . . after freedom." Ibid., p. 235. Lightly edited for readability for all ages.

Page 99: "Army men . . . citizens, it did." Boston Blackwell, Federal Writers' Project interview, Ibid., p. 29. Lightly edited for readability for all ages.

Page 100: "There were colored men . . . all my friends." Ibid., p. 29. Lightly edited for readability for all ages.

Page 100: "knew several magistrates . . ." Wylie Nealy, in Ibid., p. 236. Lightly edited for readability for all ages.

Page 102: "When I was free . . . Hampton Institute." Mary Jane Wilson, Federal Writers' Project interview in *Virginia Slave Narratives*, p. 55. Lightly edited for readability for all ages.

Page 103: "boarded with . . . my only conveniences." George W. Buckner, Federal Writers' Project interview, in *Indiana Slave Narratives* (Bedford, MA: Applewood Books; Washington, DC: Library of Congress, Print on Demand), p. 31. Lightly edited for readability for all ages.

Pages 104–105: "I never before . . . for attaining it." Charlotte Forten, quoted in McPherson, *The Negro's Civil War*, p. 119.

Page 106: "I know about . . . could devour." Charles Davenport, Federal Writers' Project interview, in *Voices from Slavery*, ed. Yetman, p. 75. Lightly edited for readability for all ages.

Page 107: "We left the plantation . . . all disappeared." Lorenzo Ezell, Federal Writers' Project interview, in Ibid., pp. 114–115. Lightly edited for readability for all ages.

Page 108: "The second swarm . . . their saddle horses." Ibid., p. 115. Lightly edited for readability for all ages.

Page 112: "the blessings . . . to the South." Rutherford B. Hayes, quoted in *The Library of Congress Civil War Desk Reference*, eds. Wagner et al., p. 795.

Pages 115–116: "Living here in Boston . . . equal in his sight." Susie King Taylor, quoted in McPherson, *The Negro's Civil War*, pp. 317–318.

Bibliography

* Indicates books suitable for children

Andrews, Charles C. *The History of New-York African Free-Schools*. New York: M. Day, 1830.

Andrews, William L., and Henry Louis Gates Jr., eds. *Slave Narratives*. New York: Library of America, 2000.

*The Anti-Slavery Alphabet. Philadelphia: Merrihew & Thompson, 1847.

Berlin, Ira, et al., eds. *Remembering Slavery: African Americans Talk about Their Personal Experiences of Slavery and Emancipation*. New York: The New Press, 1998.

*Bolden, Tonya. *Tell All the Children Our Story: Memories and Mementos of Being Young and Black in America*. New York: Abrams, 2001.

*———. *Maritcha: A Nineteenth-Century American Girl*. New York: Abrams, 2005.

*The Child's Anti-Slavery Book: Containing a Few Words about American Slave Children and Stories of Slave-Life. New York: Carlton & Porter, 1860.

Clinton, Catherine, and Nina Silber. *Divided Houses: Gender and the Civil War*. New York: Oxford University Press, 1992.

Finkelman, Paul. *Slavery in the Courtroom: An Annotated Bibliography of American Cases*. Washington, D.C.: Library of Congress, 1985.

Foner, Eric. *Reconstruction: America's Unfinished Revolution 1863–1877*. New York: Harper & Row, 1989.

Foner, Eric, and Olivia Mahoney. *America's Reconstruction: People and Politics After the Civil War*. New York: Harper Perennial, 1995.

*Frankel, Noralee. *Break Those Chains at Last: African Americans 1860–1880*. New York: Oxford University Press, 1996. (Series: Kelly, Robin D. G., and Earl Lewis, eds. *The Young Oxford History of African Americans*. New York: Oxford University Press, 1995–1997.)

Franklin, John Hope. *Reconstruction After the Civil War*. Chicago: University of Chicago Press, 1961.

*Gorrell, Gena K. *North Star to Freedom: The Story of the Underground Railroad*. New York: Delacorte Press, 1996.

Ham, Deborah Newman, ed. *The African American Odyssey*. Washington, D.C.: Library of Congress, 1998.

Jacobs, Harriet. *Incidents in the Life of a Slave Girl: Written by Herself*. Nell Irvin Painter, ed. New York: Penguin Books, 2000. (Edition of 1861 work.)

Litwack, Leon F. *Been in the Storm So Long: The Aftermath of Slavery*. New York: Knopf, 1979.

Logan, Rayford W., and Michael R. Winston, eds. *Dictionary of American Negro Biography*. New York: W.W. Norton, 1982.

Lynch, John R. *The Facts of Reconstruction*. New York: Arno Press & New York Times, 1968. (Reprint of 1913 work.)

McPherson, James M. *Marching Toward Freedom: Blacks in the Civil War 1861–1865*. New York: Facts on File, 1991.

———. *The Negro's Civil War: How American Blacks Felt and Acted During the War for the Union*. New York: Vintage Books, 2003.

*Paulson, Timothy J. *Days of Sorrow, Years of Glory 1831–1850: From the Nat Turner Revolt to the Fugitive Slave Law*. New York: Chelsea House, 1994.

*Peacock, Judith. *Reconstruction: Rebuilding After the Civil War*. Mankato, MN: Bridgestone Books, 2003.

*Pierce, Alan. *Reconstruction*. Edina, MN: ABDO Publishing Company, 2005.

Ricks, Mary Kay. *Escape on the Pearl: The Heroic Bid for Freedom on the Underground Railroad*. New York: William Morrow, 2007.

*Rogers, James T. *The Antislavery Movement*. New York: Facts on File, 1994.

Sefton, James E. *The United States Army and Reconstruction 1865–1877*. Baton Rouge: Louisiana State University Press, 1967.

Slave Narratives from the Federal Writers' Project, 1936–1938. Bedford, MA: Applewood Books; Washington, D.C.: Library of Congress. Print on Demand Series:

Alabama Slave Narratives

Arkansas Slave Narratives

Florida Slave Narratives

Georgia Slave Narratives

Indiana Slave Narratives

Kentucky Slave Narratives

Mississippi Slave Narratives

Missouri Slave Narratives

North Carolina Slave Narratives

Ohio Slave Narratives

Oklahoma Slave Narratives

South Carolina Slave Narratives

Tennessee Slave Narratives

Virginia Slave Narratives

*Smith, Carter, ed. *One Nation Again: A Sourcebook on the Civil War*. Brookfield, CT: Millbrook Press, 1993.

*Steele, Christy, and Kerry Graves, eds. *A Free Black Girl Before the Civil War: The Diary of Charlotte Forten, 1854*. Mankato, MN: Blue Earth Books, 2000.

*Stepto, Michelle, ed. *Our Song, Our Toil: The Story of American Slavery as Told by Slaves*. Brookfield, CT: Millbrook Press, 1994.

Wagner, Margaret, et al., eds. *The Library of Congress Civil War Desk Reference*. New York: Simon & Schuster, 2002.

Walker, David. *Walker's Appeal, with a Brief Sketch of His Life*. Henry Highland Garnet, ed. New York: J.H. Tobitt, 1848.

*White, Deborah Gray. *Let My People Go: African Americans 1804–1860*. New York: Oxford University Press, 1996. (Series: Kelly, Robin D. G., and Earl Lewis, eds. *The Young Oxford History of African Americans*. New York: Oxford University Press, 1995–1997.)

Winch, Julie. *A Gentleman of Color: The Life of James Forten*. New York: Oxford University Press, 2002.

Yetman, Norman, ed. *Voices from Slavery: 100 Authentic Slave Narratives*. Mineola, NY: Dover Publications, 2000.

Image Credits

All of the images in *Traveling the Freedom Road* are from the collections of the Library of Congress. Only images from the Prints and Photographs Division have negative numbers, which are indicated below. To order reproductions of images that are accompanied by a Library of Congress negative number (e.g., LC-USZ62-XXXXX; LC-USZC4-XXXXX; LC-DIG-ppmsca-XXXXX), contact the Library of Congress Photoduplication Service, Washington, D.C., 20540-4570. Telephone: (202) 707-5640; fax: (202) 707-1771; e-mail: photoduplication@loc.gov. Visit the Photoduplication Web site at http://www.loc.gov/preserv/pds/ for further information.

Key: Prints and Photographs Division = P&P; Manuscript Division = MSS; Rare Books and Special Collections Division = RBD; Geography and Maps Division = G&M; General Collections = GC.

FRONT COVER, CLOCKWISE FROM TOP LEFT
P&P, LC-USZC4-2528; P&P, LC-USZC4-2519; P&P, LC-USZ62-42791; GC; P&P, LC-USZ62-7816; P&P, LC-B8171-7890

SPINE
GC

BACK COVER, CLOCKWISE FROM TOP LEFT
P&P, LC-DIG-ppmsca-07617; P&P, LC-USZC4-973; P&P, LC-USZC4-6159

JACKET BACK FLAP
RBD

FRONTISPIECE
P&P, LC-USZ62-7357

PREFACE
Page 6: P&P, LC-DIG-ppmsca-07617

INTRODUCTION
Page 8: P&P, LC-DIG-ppmsca-04324
Page 11: P&P, LC-USZ62-89701
Page 13: MSS

SLAVERY
Page 14: P&P, LC-USZ62-104364
Page 16: P&P, LC-DIG-cwpb-03351
Page 19: P&P, LC-USZ62-44000
Page 20: P&P, LC-USZ62-54026
Page 21: P&P, LC-USZC4-2528
Page 22: P&P, LC-USZ62-2582
Page 23: P&P, LC-USZ62-77928
Page 25: P&P, LC-USZ62-103801
Page 27 top: MSS, bottom, P&P, LC-USZ62-7816
Page 28: P&P, LC-USZC4-2524
Page 29: MSS
Page 30 left: P&P, LC-USZC4-2525; right: RBD
Page 31: P&P, LC-USZC2-1329
Page 32: P&P, LC-USZC4-2356
Page 33: P&P, LC-USZ62-30803
Page 35: P&P, LC-USZC4-4659
Page 37: MSS
Page 38: GC
Page 39: RBD
Page 40: RBD
Page 41: RBD
Page 42: RBD
Page 43: P&P, LC-USZ62-7823
Page 44: P&P, LC-USZC4-8195
Page 45: P&P, LC-USZC4-3937
Page 46: P&P, LC-USZ62-132210
Page 47: GC
Page 49 top: GC; bottom: P&P, LC-USZC4-4550
Page 51: P&P, LC-USZ62-90750
Page 52: G&M
Page 53: P&P, LC-USZ62-79305
Page 55 top right: P&P, LC-USZC4-2777; bottom left: MSS

THE CIVIL WAR
Page 56: P&P, LC-B8171-152-A
Page 58: G&M

Page 59: P&P, LC-DIG-ppmsca-04325
Page 60: P&P, LC-DIG-cwpb-01549
Page 61: P&P, LC-DIG-cwpb-00218
Page 63: P&P, LC-USZ62-57025
Page 64: P&P, LC-USZC4-6158
Page 65: P&P, LC-B8184-440
Page 67: P&P, LC-USZC4-6160
Page 68: P&P, LC-USZ62-2573
Page 70: P&P, LC-USZC4-2519
Page 71 left: P&P, LC-DIG-cwpb-01699; right: P&P, LC-USZC4-6159
Page 72: P&P, LC-B8171-7890
Page 73: P&P, LC-DIG-cwpb-03756
Page 75: P&P, LC-DIG-cwpb-01929
Page 76: P&P, LC-USZC4-507

RECONSTRUCTION
Page 78: P&P, LC-B8171-3448
Page 80: P&P, LC-USZ62-8393
Page 81: P&P, LC-DIG-cwpbh-03751
Page 82: P&P, LC USZC4-4581
Pages 84–85: P&P, LC-USZC4-8109
Page 87: P&P, LC-USZC4-4575
Page 88: P&P, LC-USZ62-38843
Page 89: P&P, LC-DIG-cwpb-01823
Page 90: P&P, LC-D418-8148
Pages 92–93: P&P, LC-USZ62-89498
Page 95: P&P, LC-USZ62-42791
Page 97: P&P, LC-USZC4-973
Page 98: P&P, no negative number
Page 99: P&P, LC-USZC4-5947
Page 100: P&P, LC-USZC4-1561
Page 102: P&P, LC-USZ62-31183
Page 103: P&P, LC-USZ62-33264
Page 104: P&P, LC-USZ62-49967
Page 105: P&P, LC-USZ62-117666
Page 107: P&P, LC-USZ62-9528
Page 108: P&P, LC-USZ62-31166
Page 110: P&P, LC-USZ62-111152
Page 111: P&P, LC-USZ62-87440
Page 113: P&P, LC-USZ62-107719
Page 114: P&P, LC-USZC4-2851
Page 115: P&P, LC-USZ62-78481
Page 117: P&P, LC-USZ62-119595

Acknowledgments

Many thanks go to the people who helped to make *Traveling the Freedom Road* possible. Ralph Eubanks, Director of the Library of Congress Publishing Office, shared his enthusiasm for this project from its beginning, and Acting Director John Cole and Peggy Wagner have given it continued support. My editor at Abrams, Howard Reeves, has made invaluable suggestions to enrich the text and illustrations and has been a pleasure to work with. Thanks, too, to Scott Auerbach, associate managing editor, and copy editor Diane Aronson for their careful attention to the manuscript, and to Maggie Lehrman for her assistance. Maria T. Middleton helped this book come alive with her elegant, impressive design.

I researched this book in many divisions of the Library of Congress. I appreciate the help of staff in the Prints and Photographs, Manuscript, Rare Books and Special Collections, and Geography and Maps Divisions, as well as the Photoduplication Service. The other writers, editors, and staff of the Publishing Office were always ready with splendid ideas and encouragement: Aimee Hess, Blaine Marshall, Susan Reyburn, Myint Myint San, Evelyn Sinclair, Anji Keating, and Vincent Virga. Special thanks to Wilson McBee for his skill and organization in handling the copying of nineteenth-century book pages. I am also grateful to Casey King, who inspired me to learn and write about African American history.

Finally, tremendous thanks to my husband, Bob, and daughter, Catherine, who read and reread the manuscript, listened to many hours of deliberation, and were there for every discovery and insight; and to my son, Nick, a graduate student in American history, who unfailingly improved *Freedom Road* by sharing his knowledge, humor, and love of the subject.

Index

Page numbers in italics refer to illustrations

Mexican-American War, 48, 118
Mexico, land gained from, 48, *49*, 118
Milliken's Bend, Louisiana, 75
Mississippi, 21, 54, 101, 109, 118, 119
Mississippi River, 23, *114*
Missouri, 54
Missouri Compromise, 24, 118
Moseley, Isom, 91–92
Moss, Andrew, 79
Mount Airy, Louisiana, *22*
Myrtilla Miner's School for Free Colored Girls, 7, 54, *55*

N

Narrative of Frederick Douglass, 118
Nashville, Tennessee, 64
Nast, Thomas, *68*
National Association for the Advancement of Colored People (NAACP), 119
National Equal Rights League, 119
Nealy, Wylie, 98, 99, 100
Nebraska, 52
Nevada, 48
New Bern, North Carolina, 62, 82, 104
New Mexico, 48
New Orleans, Louisiana, 83, *113*
New-York African Free-Schools, *38*, 39
North Carolina, 54, *82*, 83, 104, *107*, 119
North Star, 43

O

Oberlin, Ohio, 17
O'Sullivan, Timothy, *56*
Ocean Waves (ship), 62

P

Pearl (schooner), 15–16
Pennsylvania Anti-Slavery Society, 34
Petersburg, Virginia, 77
Philadelphia, 15, *27*, 34, 36
Pinchback, P. B. S., *100*, 101
Plessy v. Ferguson, 119
Port Hudson, Louisiana, 75
Port Republic, Battle of, 66
Portsmouth, Virginia, 102
Preliminary Emancipation Proclamation, 118

Q

Quakers, 43

R

racism, 10
    and Civil War, 58
    persistence of, 119
    resurgence of, 106–09
    in Union army, 73–75
Radical Republicans, 82
Rainey, Joseph, *100*, 101, 119
Randall, Millie, 96
Rawlings, John A., *71*
Reconstruction, 79–80
    African American attitudes during, 86–92
    African American role in, 83–84
    aftermath of, 116–18, *118*
    anti-black violence during, 83, *110*
    economic issues during, 91–92
    educational opportunities afforded by, 105, *105*

    end of, 111–13, *113*, *114*, 119
    land redistribution during, 91–92
    military role in, 83–84
    southern state politics in, 81–82
Reconstruction Acts, 119
Republican Party, 48, 118
Revels, Hiram, 101, 119
Richmond, Virginia, 77, *102*
Roanoke, Virginia, 62
Robinson, Tom, 86
Rock, John, 45

S

St. Phillip's Church, *102*
Salem, Massachusetts, 38
Savannah, Georgia, *98*
Scott, Dred, 52, 96, 118
    family of, *53*
Scott v. Sanford, 52, 118
secession, 54, 57, *58*, 118
Second Rhode Island Volunteer Infantry, *64*
segregation, *114*, 119
separate but equal doctrine, 119
sharecroppers, *90*, 91–92, *93*
Sharpsburg, Maryland, 66
Shaw, Robert Gould, 76, *76*
Sherman, William Tecumseh, 91, 119
Shiloh, Battle of, 66
Sidney, Thomas, 39
Simmons, Eveleen, 40
Slaughter, Richard, 73, 74
slave ships, *19*
slave trade, 11–12, *11*, *16*, 22–23, *23*, 48, 118
slavery
    abolition of, 13
    in American colonies, 10
    during Civil War, 59, 62
    economics of, 17, *21*
    eyewitness testimony about, 24–27
    history of, 11–12
    legacy of, 9
    as political issue, 23–25
    in United States, 12
slaves
    children as, 30–31
    conditions of, *22*, 24–26, 28
    depicted in art, *25*, *27*, *28*, *32*
    educational oppression of, 29
    escape attempts of, 15–17, 30, *32*, 33–34, 62–64
    excuses made for, 32
    freedom opportunities for, 33, 34
    legal status of, 28
    physical abuse of, 26, 28
    as property, 11, 30–31
    relations with owners, *31*
    separation of families, 30, *31*
Smith's Plantation, *56*
South America, 45
South Carolina, *8*, 35, 54, 55, *56*, *59*, 76, *76*, 77, 78, 95, 101, *105*, 112, *113*, 118, 119
states' rights, 57
Stephens, Alexander, 58
Stevens, Thaddeus, 82
Stewart, Maria, 43
Sumner, Charles, 82
Suttle, Charles, 50